TURN YOUR FEAR INTO FUEL

PRAISE FOR JOHN ADDISON & REAL LEADERSHIP VOLUME 2

"John's nine simple practices are straightforward and backed by real-life experience. His words will motivate you to lead and live with courage, honor, and integrity."
—David Bach, *New York Times* bestselling author of *The Automatic Millionaire* and *Start Late, Finish Rich*

"True leaders inspire others to lead. John Addison is that kind of leader, inspiring the next generation of leaders using ageless wisdom, modern examples, and practical tools. Positive leadership is practiced, not inherited."
—Shawn Achor, *New York Times* bestselling author of *The Happiness Advantage*

"John Addison is more than a leader, he's a coach and a motivator."
—Jack Canfield, *New York Times* bestselling author of *The Success Principles* and the *Chicken Soup for the Soul* series.

"[*Real Leadership*] is a fascinating and deeply personal account of three decades of success in facing challenges and surmounting obstacles, filled with powerful anecdotes and inspiration from great leaders of the past."
—Lee Pollock, Executive Director, The Churchill Centre

ALSO BY JOHN ADDISON

Real Leadership Volume 2: 9 Simple Practices for Leading and Living With Purpose

Addisonisms: Quotes to Live By

Never Take Advice from Anyone More Screwed Up Than You Are

Check Your Shocks: Secrets to Creating a Legacy of Leadership

TURN YOUR FEAR INTO FUEL

JOHN ADDISON

© 2025 Addison Leadership Group, Inc.

All rights reserved. Published by Addison Leadership Group, Inc., Gainesville, GA

Turn Your Fear Into Fuel by John Addison

First edition, 2025

ISBN: 978-1-7355991-5-1

Photo credits: John Addison

Design & Pagination: The Cognitive Creative, LLC

For my wonderful family. True success is a happy family.

To everyone who wants to do something great in life, but is held back by fear, uncertainty, or doubt.

ACKNOWLEDGMENTS

First, I would like to dedicate this book to my family. Loveanne and I have been blessed with a wonderful life of joy and happiness. We have been married for forty-three years, and we have amazing friends with whom we share great adventures at home and on our many travels. We have wonderful children and grandchildren. Thank you to Kyle, Di, Kai and Luka; and Tyler, Emily, James and Ruth who bring so much happiness and fulfillment to our lives. Grandchildren are a true gift of joy!

I want to thank my Primerica team and family. The true joy of my business life was being a part of that team! Rick Williams, my friend and business partner, and I had the honor of leading Primerica to the triumph of freedom and independence after the financial crisis of 2008. I am proud of the company's continued soaring success under the leadership of Glenn Williams and his team. Primerica truly has the greatest group of field leaders of any company in the world!

It is a true honor to work with the leaders of LegalShield, Utility Warehouse, Ambit Energy, and so many wonderful companies who believe in delivering amazing products and allowing people to live their dreams.

I want to thank Dayna Stuckey, my true right-hand person, who has the impossible job of keeping me organized.

To Tess, Lacey, Leann, Sydney, Mandy, and the team at The Cognitive Creative, this book would be scratched words on one of my notepads without your creativity and driving force. Thank you.

Finally, to you, my readers. My humble thanks to you for reading my words. I hope you find them useful on your quest to succeed in life despite what scares you. I owe my own success in life to the ideas, efforts, and successes of countless others. Without the positive power of uncertainty which taught me empathy and the ability to embrace others' ideas, I would not be here.

I will see you at the top because the bottom sure is crowded.

John Addison

CONTENTS

	Prologue	1
1.	Self-Doubt Is Only the Beginning	7
2.	Fear Is a Thief	17
3.	Uncertainty Wears Many Faces	27
4.	Courage Is Not Comfortable	39
5.	Tactical Thinking	55
6.	The Art of Gratitude	69
7.	Commit to the Journey	83
8.	A Bias for Action	93
9.	Flipping the Script on Fear	107
10.	What is Required	125
11.	The Bountiful Balance	143
12.	Action This Day	157
	Epilogue	169
	About the Author	177

PROLOGUE

Biology teaches us that we are human beings. I have a different take on that, particularly when it comes to success and achieving our goals.

I believe the secret to getting where we want to go in life is to view ourselves not as human beings, but as *human becomings.* Every day, we are either improving or we are getting worse. We don't stay the same. We have to live life with the mindset of becoming and being better. I wrote this book for people who want to do something with their life. It is for those who aren't satisfied to merely exist. It's for those who want to make a difference, but may have these gnawing little insecurities and doubts—*Am I smart enough? Do I have what it takes? Am I wearing the right shoes?*—that can hold them back.

I decided to write this book because the vast majority of people I have encountered are hard-wired to be fearful and to cast doubt on themselves, myself included. Whatever you are afraid of, whatever compelled you to pick up this book, I promise you that I have been equally scared. There are days that I am still scared. I have just learned to accept that fear, doubt, and uncertainty are all essential to life. I've learned to make fear and doubt integral to action, because action begets success.

In case you don't know—I'm a country boy. I was raised in Covington, Georgia. My childhood was charmed. We were not wealthy, but we had all of the things that make life worth living. When you grow up in the rural South, you don't know that you're different until you know that you're different.

In elementary school and later in high school, I had the same insecurities as my peers. Of course, we didn't share those fears with each other, and none of us thought the other felt the same way. If nothing else I say sticks, please understand this: *The vast majority of us are burdened with doubt.* We are challenged by insecurity and we are afraid. Some of us rise above challenges, and some of us fall victim to them. And, there are times in which you will do both. You will rise above some fears, and others will stop you in your tracks and stomp a mudhole in you. I know this because, in spite of my success, I have both triumphed over doubt and been trampled by it.

In 1975, I left home to attend the University of Georgia. Covington, where I grew up, and Athens, Georgia, are not too far apart as the crow flies; but with the difference in culture, I might as well have been in Paris, France. My excitement to attend UGA was unwavering; it was a dream come true. My fears about my ability to fit in, excel, and not get laughed right back to my parents' house, well … those, too, were unwavering.

I questioned everything about myself. I didn't feel smart enough, and I was sure I wasn't dressed right. I just knew I was somehow less than I needed to be. These types of fears can paralyze you. I found UGA to be big and daunting, and I wanted to quit. Not just UGA, but college in general—so much so in fact that my parents convinced me to enroll at the much smaller Oxford College of Emory University in the winter quarter of my freshman year. After finding my feet at Oxford I was able to return to UGA as a Junior with far less insecurity. I settled in and ended up making better grades than the kids with the designer clothes and fancy cars.

You might think the success I ultimately found in college would forge me for the future. Not so.

I still recall the first time I sat in a New York City boardroom. Stacks of papers in neat folders sat on the large, gleaming conference table in front of men with expensive haircuts and even more expensive suits. By this point, I had certainly climbed the corporate ladder and—by anyone else's standards but my own—I deserved a seat at that table. I was knowledgeable and skilled enough to go toe-to-toe with anyone there. But that's not what my brain told me.

When you are fearful that you don't belong and that you aren't enough, you should at least be given some type of imagination award for the creative bull crap your mind comes up with. Suddenly, your tie clip is at the axis of your destruction. Oh, and your choice of shoes, which are tucked under the table as you try to hide them for not being Italian enough, is surely grounds for dismissal without severance.

I exaggerate here for thematic effect, but honestly, not by much. I have lamented everything from my accent to why I ordered lasagna during a business lunch. Thankfully, none of the wild scenarios from my mental gymnastics have ever come to pass.

The truth is, most of the powerful and successful people I know are also some of the most insecure. Typically, when someone acts "too confident," it's because they are, in fact, insecure. Successful people never truly vanquish their fears; they just learn to recognize them and overcome them. They have learned that while self-doubt may feel like the enemy, it is often a necessary evil that can be used for good when harnessed correctly.

When I was a youngster, I took tennis lessons from a retired top-ranked player named Miss Louise Fowler who lived in our area. When we would travel to play in tournaments around

Georgia, often the kids I played against were Old Atlanta Buckhead Money, not Covington Money. They were from families whose last names are etched in the history of Georgia in banking, broadcasting, manufacturing, and more. I like to say these kids were born on third base and thought they hit a triple to get there. They were set up for success.

At the time, I couldn't put my finger on why I felt slightly out of place next to them, why they brought up some sort of insecurity in me. I had to grow up a little to finally figure it out.

It was intimidating to be around those wealthy kids. I didn't go to all the right schools like they did. I didn't wear the latest fashion. My teeth weren't perfectly straight and white. And, although I was a good little athlete, I didn't have the financial backing they did to see me to the top of a sports bracket. I was from a middle class home in the country. I was a little scared, slightly lumpy, insecure, and imperfect.

So, if you have ever felt like I did at that tennis club, or at UGA, or in that boardroom, I want you to know that this book is for you.

If you get up every day and think about how you have fallen short but want to do better, then I wrote it for you.

If you feel insecure and as though you have challenging circumstances to overcome, this book is also for you.

If you have a burning desire to do something great, and you know you have what it takes to overcome the fear that's trying to stop you dead in your tracks, then every single word in this book was written for YOU.

On the flip side, if you are a person who already thinks you are perfect and never wrong, or that you're the smartest person in any room you enter, this book is not for you. Obviously you have already arrived and probably won't be interested in what I have to say anyway.

But I'm willing to bet that you and I are not very different from each other—we *both* have fears and doubts. The only difference is that, somewhere along the way, I learned to use my fears to fuel my growth and my success. That's the impetus for this book: to comfort you, inform you, guide you, and empower you to use fear and uncertainty to fuel growth, further knowledge, and push boundaries. My sincere hope is that you will learn enough about flipping the narrative on doubt and fear to turn your dreams into goals and then make those goals your reality.

Read to get to work? Let's do it.

1

SELF-DOUBT IS ONLY THE BEGINNING

"I'll see you at the top because the bottom sure is crowded."

I close my keynote speeches, videos for my website, and letters with those words.

Stop for a moment to think about why the bottom might be crowded. Why is the top less so?

I believe it's because most people doubt that they can ever *get* to the top. They see it as a pipe dream. It's a little like answering the question, "What's the first thing you'd do if you won the lottery?" with no intention of ever playing the lottery. Folks daydream about a lifestyle that reflects wealth and status, but fear and doubt prevent them from believing that they can achieve their dreams. Dreams stay dreams, rather than becoming goals to pursue.

At some point, we have all been gripped with the fear that we aren't enough. If ever there were a litmus test for being "normal," occasionally succumbing to our insecurities is it. I have woken in the middle of the night, inexplicably white-knuckled with the fear that I was somehow incapable of tackling the day ahead. Our minds are often riddled with these doubt-fueled self-judgements: I am not good enough, I am not smart enough, I am out of my depth.

I'm sure you could add your own late-night mutterings to the list.

It starts early, too. In adolescence, we are all live wires of insecurity walking around middle and high school campuses trying desperately to fit in. Are we wearing the right clothes? Are we tall enough, or are we too tall? Are we cute enough? Do the other kids even like us?

You're not just programmed with fear; you're likely an involuntary, card-carrying member of the Irrational Fears Club. And guess what? You should count your blessings that you are! While that card is heavy, and often you wish you didn't have to hold on to it, it is necessary if you want to become a successful leader and a strong human being.

Yes, you read that right. Fear and doubt can be uncomfortable, painful, and even downright unbearable; however, these feelings are necessities in life and success. Why? Because self-doubt gives us perspective. It leads to empathy and understanding of the fears and insecurities of others. If you think you are one-hundred percent right one-hundred percent of the time, not only are you probably not much fun to be around, you are closing yourself off to learning and growing and the deep satisfaction that comes with being able to relate to others.

Self-doubt is not the end of the road for your goals and dreams, it is only the beginning. It is the necessary ingredient to fuel your journey forward. The juxtaposition of doubt and confidence is what motivates so many people (including yours truly) to step outside of their comfort zone and achieve what was once only a pipe dream. Without doubt, confidence is empty and meaningless. They are two sides of the same coin.

LET'S FACE IT: WE'RE ALL FIVE YEARS OLD

It has been said that most of the doubts, fears, and anxieties we struggle with as adults are programmed in our psyches by the time we are five years old. After all, fear is instilled early as a biological safety mechanism. It is meant to keep us alive. But what if we could stop it early on? Would it make us more well-adjusted and productive adults?

As a young man just out of college, I entered the insurance industry. When I started at A.L. Williams & Associates, I was twenty-five years old and certain that I wouldn't stay there long. It was a pit stop on the way to my MBA and future as a consultant. Boy, was I wrong. Over the next thirty years, I rose through the ranks of the company that would become Primerica, eventually serving as co-CEO with Rick Williams. Together with our incredible sales force and amazing home office team, we successfully weathered the worst financial collapse in decades and led Primerica to a super successful IPO.

During my early days at the company, the founder, Art Williams, held regular meetings in hotel ballrooms in Atlanta that opened my eyes to the power of communication and personal growth. Art spoke to a crowd of two thousand insurance salesmen like no one I had ever seen. His ability to communicate from the stage and really reach us on a heart-level was unparalleled in my book. He understood that everyone has struggles, fears, and personal hurdles on the road to success.

Occasionally, Art would invite a business associate named Stanley Beyer to speak to us. Stanley was the CEO of PennCorp Financial, the underwriter for the insurance policies that our company sold. He would stand on stage and talk to us about fears, explaining that we are all walking around in turmoil with our very own inner child.

He had a point. Have you ever tried to talk a five-year-old out of an irrational fear? I'm here to tell you, as a father of two, that is a long row to hoe. When one of our boys was convinced a monster was under the bed, neither my wife, Loveanne, nor I, could erase his fear completely, even with all the love, trust, and gentleness imaginable.

Well, as Stanley told us, we are always and forever battling with that scared inner five-year-old. With any other five-year-old, we'd be kind and gentle, but we're not usually very gentle with ourselves. We beat ourselves up. We tell ourselves the self-doubt is right, that we aren't good enough or strong enough or talented enough and that failure and public embarrassment are imminent. We say things to ourselves we would never say out loud to another human being, let alone a child.

Instead of continuing this battle, think about this: Have you considered using doubt and fear to propel you to your next goal? After all, tapping into that fear can be useful. It informs our nervous system of danger so we recognize and watch for it in the real world. Yet, biologically viable as it may be, this fear can still cripple us if we let it.

So, is managing that fear and doubt a simple task? No.

Knowing a fear isn't real and experiencing it that way—*feeling* that it isn't real—are two very different things. Sometimes, we have to just try to use it to our advantage.

TOUGH AS DICKENS

I have been a student of fear and doubt for a while now. I've watched documentaries, read books, and dealt with it firsthand more times than I can count. I've also tried to take lessons from the lives of historical figures and great leaders who I admire.

I love the writings of Charles Dickens. I have his whole collection on the library wall in my office, and every year at Christmas time, I re-read *A Christmas Carol*. Charles Dickens is arguably one of the most famous writers of all time. He's also someone who used the fears of his early life to his advantage later in life. One of eight children, Dickens dreamed of a bright future for himself. He desperately wanted to become educated, but only his sister Fanny was allowed to complete her formal education. Instead, after his father went to debtors' prison, Dickens went to work in a factory at age twelve and stopped school altogether at fifteen.

Undoubtedly, Dickens struggled into adulthood with the challenges of his youth. I imagine his inner five-year-old voice was a frequent reminder of his incomplete education, lack of training, and everything a successful writer "should" be. At the same time, somehow, he took those hardships and used them to stoke the embers of his undeniable talent. His experiences fueled his creative fires. I suspect his inner child's voice of determination gave him the drive to write so many beloved classics. Without Dickens' hardships and self-doubt, we would never have *Oliver Twist* or *David Copperfield*, both inspired by his childhood experiences and fears.

There's a little-known story about one of my heroes, Sir Winston Churchill, that also illustrates Stanley Beyer's point about the fears of our inner child still dogging us from within.

Unlike Dickens, Churchill grew up with means, thanks to his mother. His father was an aristocrat and former Chancellor of the House of Commons. However, with the aristocracy running low on funds, the elder Churchill solved that problem by marrying a beautiful American heiress.

As a child, Churchill didn't seem bound for greatness. He was not the favorite son. That honor went to his younger brother, Jack. At best, Winston's relationship with both of his parents was complex, and it often left him shrouded in doubt. He was an average student, often described as clumsy and unimpressive. Later, he struggled to gain admittance to the Royal Military Academy Sandhurst, in the United Kingdom.

During his first year as a cadet, he accidentally dropped a treasured gift from his father, a valuable gold pocket watch, into a nearby stream. This gift was so precious that Churchill stripped down and braved frigid water in the desperate hope of finding his watch. While he was unsuccessful, he wasn't deterred. He hired twenty-three members of his infantry detachment to dig trenches to reroute the stream so that the pool of water his watch fell into would drain away. Then, he borrowed the school's fire engine and pumped the streambed completely dry.

Finally, there at the bottom was his watch. It was in sad disrepair, full of rust and silt. Churchill made arrangements and sent the watch back to the maker to be taken apart, cleaned, and returned to him.

As fate would have it, his father visited the watchmaker's shop during the repair and learned of the watch's icy plunge. Churchill's father wrote to him and berated him for his irresponsibility:

"It is clear you are not to be trusted with a valuable watch, and when I get it from Mr. Dent, I shall not give it back to you. You had better buy one of those cheap watches for £ 2 as those are the only ones, which, if you smash, are not very costly to replace. Jack has had the watch I gave him longer than you have had yours; the only expenses I have paid on his watch were for cleanings before he went back to Harrow. But in all qualities of steadiness, taking care of his things, and never doing stupid things, Jack is vastly your superior."

True to his word, Churchill's father gave the watch to Jack, and Winston never again carried it.

Later in life, he said that he could only recall three or four long and intimate conversations with his father. In 1947 he wrote a short story called "The Dream," in which he was visited by the ghost of his father. In the dream, his father asks, "What has happened since I died?" Churchill spoke at length with his father, telling him about the world, the rise of fascism, and all that had transpired since his father had passed away. Yet, before he could tell him that he became prime minister, helped save the world, or that he was considered a world-class leader, his father vanished.

Even the greatest heroes have demons they struggle to keep at bay.

I have been fortunate to travel to London and learn about the life of Winston Churchill in depth. I've been in the Cabinet War Rooms and felt the well-worn groove in the arm of his chair caused by the repetitive tapping of his signet ring. I have to wonder if the nervous gesture that caused the groove in the sturdy oak of that chair had its beginnings in the self-doubts of a much younger man.

Thank God Winston Churchill managed to wrestle his inner child into submission so he could save the world from hell.

DON'T WATER THE KUDZU

If you are from the South, you've heard of kudzu. If you're not familiar, it's an invasive vine that was imported here to help with erosion. This stuff is a menace. If you blink, it grows three feet. It eats the land. I've even seen it totally consume a house. It reminds me of fear, the way it grows on its own without the need for cultivation. If you watered it, it would take over like wildfire.

Kudzu also has tons of benefits. It's been used for millennia in Chinese medicine, and today Chinese doctors are using a chemical found in kudzu to treat stroke and blood clots. Top Western medical institutes like Memorial Sloan Kettering Cancer Center and Harvard report positive health benefits from kudzu roots and flowers. It turns out that "the vine that ate the South" can improve and maybe even save your life. Who would have thought that something so bothersome could be such a blessing?

You can't really conquer kudzu, as it is super invasive and prolific. But you can tame it. You can harvest the root and make a tea that has a host of benefits. This is also the case with self-doubt. You can learn to tame it and extract from it what you need to propel you forward.

The secret truth about "conquering" those inner fears is that you don't. You wrestle with self-doubt and stand toe-to-toe with it, but it is an unwavering foe. It's a shapeshifter that appears at inopportune times. You can, however, flip the script on the feelings of inadequacy and doubt that have plagued you and stopped you from moving forward. That's what this book is all about. I hope to help you convert your fears into rocket fuel—or, as in the case of kudzu, a recipe for your next steps.

NO MAGIC BULLET

Before we go any further, I need to make one thing clear. Please do not make the mistake of thinking I figured out how to quash all my fears and that's how I achieved what I have in life. This couldn't be further from the truth.

Yes, I reached the highest level of leadership at an extremely successful public financial services company. I worked hard to get where I was with Primerica. I had done well in school, graduating the University of Georgia cum laude and earning my MBA from George State University with honors. But when I walked into a boardroom full of Ivy League-bred, Wall Street-trained executives, the voice in my head wasn't reminding me that my degrees were from good schools or that I was an experienced professional with a lot to add to the conversation.

Instead, that old self-doubt started pointing out all the ways I didn't measure up. Even my accent was a giveaway that I was an outsider when it came to the Wall Street club. I had to decide right then and there what to do about that voice. Listen to it and keep my mouth shut at a meeting where the well-being of our company was on the line? Or make a different choice and let that fear fire me up?

There is no magic pill in the pages of this book to help you ala-ka-zam your way to fearlessness. I am a straight shooter, so I'll tell you now: There is no workaround, no easy way to deal with the doubts that we all have. What I want you to see is that you can acknowledge your fear, harness it, and eventually use it to your advantage.

So, if you can't avoid fear and self-doubt, if there's no magic bullet and no easy workaround, how can you succeed?

To start with, you accept the fact that your fears aren't going anywhere. You are stuck with them, just like I am. You are not the only person to struggle with self-doubt, anxiety, fear, or even self-loathing. We have all felt like an imposter in our own lives, like we were tricking the world into thinking we know what we're doing when we don't. But the self-doubts we're all saddled with are just the beginning, not the end. The idea is to stop leaning into them. Let's focus on what you should lean into instead.

The truth is, along with all the fear and self-doubt, you also have very real talents and skills. You have experience, intelligence, and abilities that have already enabled you to accomplish goals. These positive attributes aren't going anywhere! They don't disappear just because you feel afraid you might fail.

So let me be clear: You are not a phony. I know this because you wouldn't have bought a book to help you in a fear-wrestling contest if you were a fake.

Just like anything else you've learned to do, learning to use your fear to your advantage requires your attention and your intention. If you intend to boost your potential with your fears, you will get an entirely different outcome than if you intend to give into them. Reading this book shows you already have the right intention.

So, let's turn our attention to converting that fear into rocket fuel.

2

FEAR IS A THIEF

Is fear ingrained in us from birth? It is said, and research reveals, that we are born with both a fear of falling and a fear of loud noises. So, the short answer is yes, fear is with us when we are born. Beyond those two, fears are learned.

In many cases, I think fears can also be imagined. This goes for both rational and irrational fears. After all, when you're born, you aren't aware that spiders and snakes could pose a danger to you. Your attitude toward the natural world is more likely to be formed by others and their experiences.

I admit openly and without reservation that I am irrationally terrified of snakes. Where you see a branch fall from a tree, I see a copperhead. When you hear a rustle of leaves and assume it's a squirrel, I am convinced it's a timber rattler. You might call it paranoia. I prefer hyper-vigilance.

Still, I am aware that my fear is out of bounds with even the most avid woodsman's average number of snake encounters. My imagination jumps in and things can seem more dangerous than they really are.

Where did this fear come from? I wasn't born with it. Maybe

it has to do with an overabundance of snake-themed problems on *Gunsmoke*, or Johnny Weissmuller as Tarzan wrestling giant boa constrictors on Saturday mornings when I was a kid. More probable is that someone close to me in my developmental years had an irrational fear and a vivid imagination too.

Fear, of course, can be rational. I am afraid of heights, and there is no way on God's earth that I would jump out of an airplane. I am aware that most people do not die from this activity. Still, I think my fear is pretty rational. The fear factor of skydiving far outweighs any fun I could even begin to have while jumping out of a plane.

When fear is rational, it's a little easier to deal with. Afraid of falling asleep during a meeting? Stop staying up so late. Afraid of stumbling over your words during your presentation? Rehearse it until it becomes natural.

Most of the time, irrational fears are the ones that keep us from taking action and hold us back from being productive and successful in life. These are the fears that no one else could reasonably foresee happening, but you can't shake the thought of it being a possibility.

I promise you that I duked it out with fear more times as co-CEO of Primerica than I ever did climbing the ladder. In leadership, it's pretty common to get tripped up in fear. People are paying attention, so you worry that you're not smart enough, or articulate enough, or strong enough to shoulder the burdens. This list is long. I can fill the whole book with reasons I have been afraid. More often than not, I made those reasons up in my head, and they weren't even warranted.

GUMPTION TRAPS

If you have read Robert M. Pirsig's classic autobiographical novel *Zen and the Art of Motorcycle Maintenance: An Inquiry into Values*, you know it's not about Buddhism or how to tune up a Honda

Super Hawk. Rather, it is the story of a father and his son on a cross-country trip. The dialogue dabbles in philosophy and romanticism, and it even nods to concepts found in the works of Friedrich Nietzsche.

I first read *Zen and the Art of Motorcycle Maintenance* in a philosophy class while at Oxford College of Emory University. Pirsig's writing helped me recognize the correlation between fear and achievement.

What the book cleverly accomplishes is the identification of two distinct personality types. Pirsig gives us the gestalt, an in-the-moment romanticist who isn't at all analytical, and his polar opposite, a critical thinker who needs all the details and inner workings. One character enjoys maintaining his motorcycle and has a deep understanding of mechanics. The other couldn't care less about upkeep and considers mechanical knowledge a waste of brainpower.

I use this book and the personality types in it as examples because both personalities deal with fear, just different types of fear. We are all connected in our fears and are only separated by what we fear and how we choose to handle it.

Pirsig didn't think his book would amount to much. In fact, it was rejected one hundred and twenty-one times before an editor agreed to publish it. The initial sales for *Zen and the Art of Motorcycle Maintenance* eclipsed five million copies. It was a bestseller for decades and today is often required reading in high school literature classes.

Pirsig coined a term that I think applies to working alongside your fear that he called a "gumption trap." A gumption trap is an event or a state of mind that causes a person to lose enthusiasm or become discouraged from finishing or even starting a project. In other words, they make you lose your gumption—your resourceful determination.

Gumption traps are, in essence, negative feedback loops—highlight reels of our possible failures and inadequacies. *Zen and the Art of Motorcycle Maintenance* helps cement the understanding that we create our fears. Actually, we tailor them, but unlike an expensive suit, we tailor them on the fly.

The mind does not need much time to create a perfectly personal and highly intimate fear that we internalize as truth. We indoctrinate ourselves with what we perceive as our worst qualities. We relive our past failures in gory detail. We lament all unknown variables and anything else generally negative that will halt our progress. Our brains are exceedingly good at this.

I've observed that the further you go in life without facing fear, the bigger the rut you dig for yourself without even realizing it. This rut you create not only keeps you down but can also work against you as an emotional blinder to opportunities.

If you don't escape that gumption trap, you won't recognize good fortune, even if it slaps you in the face.

My hope is to help you avoid those gumption traps and assist you in creating internal feedback that elevates and supports your success rather than holding you prisoner in your mind. It's not easy. I will warn you: At times, it's going to be scary. But I would wager that it will also be entirely worth it once you see your way beyond fear to your first major achievement. This is life-changing stuff.

FEAR IS A THIEF

Let's talk about progress, or the lack thereof. You need to know that fear is a thief. You might do well to write that simple, four-word statement down.

Fear. Is. A. Thief.

You got that?

I'd like you to think for just a moment about the people in your life up to this point. Think about their talent and ideas and their ability to act. Chances are, you know people who stepped out in faith and did something scary. It's also highly likely you know someone who was amazingly talented but who left the world with their music still inside them. Fear robbed them of their chance to share their gift with the world.

Fear is a thief. We can't progress without taking action, but we won't act when fear paralyzes us. Don't allow fear to steal from you. You can choose to act, despite what scares you.

Doing nothing, choosing purposefully to stay in your comfort zone, is just as much of a decision as bold action. Think about it: Inaction is intentional. If what you focus on grows, then a deliberate decision to stay idle is an exercise in stagnation.

You aren't simply sitting on the bench without an opportunity to play. You are actively giving your turn away to the thief.

What future achievements that are nowhere near being on your radar might be thwarted if fear wins today?

You don't need to constantly fret and develop paranoia that your present self is going to ruin things for your future self. That's not productive. However, when you consider all the directions our lives can take and the roads we will go down, it's the roads we don't go down that probably have the most lasting negative impact. Namely, regret.

The fears that stop us in our tracks or keep us from ever getting started are mental mutterings that pull us away from our goals. (They are 100% gumption traps.) You will put off making a decision to act out of a need for more information or more time or more preparation.

Let me tell you: You will never have all of the information you need in the formats you need it in.

It will probably never be the "perfect time."

Life will not grant you the space you think you need to do your best work.

The truth is, you will always be your most clever when finding a way to avoid decisions and taking action. The ego will see to this. For the tough questions in life, there are no easy answers. That's not to say you shouldn't do your due diligence, but there is a big difference between research and running in circles.

There is a lot in this world you cannot control. You can, however, control the actions you take. Don't let fear rob you of your opportunities to act in the moment. When you can take action, grab the opportunity!

AIM AND ADJUST

I ran a large company for years. We had a massive salesforce consisting of an amazing group of smart, strong, and talented individuals. When you have a large group of intelligent and opinionated folks, there is no such thing as consensus. Ideas and opinions vary wildly. All I could do was listen with discernment and try to be a bridge among the people whose opinions I most valued. Then it was my job to understand and weigh any long-term consequences of the decisions I made.

Ultimately, no matter what, I had to take action. I wasn't always sure, I wasn't always on target, and I missed the mark now and then. Sometimes you will miss the target too. That's okay. There's no reason to throw your bow and arrows in the trash and walk away. Sometimes, it is only when you miss the mark that what you really need to do to hit that bull's-eye becomes obvious.

Only after we've done it wrong can we see how to do it right.

The idea of quitting is a funny thing. Our society ridicules quitters and I don't advocate for it myself. Yet, like so many things in life, it's all in how you look at it. Even a person who quits is, at minimum, a person who begins. So which is worse: missing the mark, quitting, or not acting at all?

I have wanted to quit more than once in my life.

I wanted to quit college. I was turning over rocks for any good reason to leave the University of Georgia. Don't get me wrong, I love my Bulldogs. On the one hand, I was such a fan and I was proud to be there. On the other hand, I felt out of place.

Back home, I had a girlfriend, a job, and a bad-to-the-bone car, a '69 Chevelle. I was well-liked and comfortable. At UGA, I was no longer a big deal. There were 25,000 students, and I was lost in a sea of people who seemed smarter, savvier, and far more at ease than I was.

Quitting was heavy on my mind. In my book, *Real Leadership*, I tell the story of one of my professors referring to the class syllabus. If you've read it, you might recall that I had no clue what a "syllabus" was. So, to say that I felt inadequate is a gross understatement.

Fortunately, my mom and dad convinced me to transfer as a freshman to Oxford College of Emory University. It was closer to home and smaller. There, the average class size was only ten or twelve students. I was immediately more comfortable, and my confidence grew as I realized that I had the opportunity to be competitive academically while still being comfortable socially. Oxford drew very bright students from all over the United States. It was there that I discovered my potential. When I believed I was just as smart and capable as my peers, I grew bolder.

My time there set me up for success when I returned to UGA in my junior year. I truly loved those next two years as a Bulldog. Empowered, I was no longer allowing fear to run my life.

It had required making a change that, at the time, might have looked like quitting. I had made a small deviation from my bigger plan of graduating from UGA. But I didn't quit altogether.

I aimed and adjusted. This pivot helped me maintain the sense that I was succeeding and moving forward. I hadn't failed. I made a change that worked better for me at the time.

Years later, the flames of my insecurities and fears were sometimes fanned during the transitions that my company, A.L. Williams, went through on the way to becoming Primerica. Change, though inevitable, is never easy. During this time, the fear I felt was reminiscent of those early days at UGA. I felt out of place, and I thought of leaving.

We all have those moments in which fear grips us. It might be the fear that we aren't enough, or it could be the fear that we are missing out on something better. Although I was tempted to pack up and leave on more than one occasion, I didn't. Instead, I decided to face the fears, the challenges, and the uncertainty, and fortunately, I stayed at Primerica.

That turned out to be one of the most critical decisions of my life. I would not be who I am today had I let the fear deter me. In fact, you would not be reading these words. Interesting to think about, isn't it?

The secret is to aim and adjust, to play chess with your fears. Admittedly, I was not gifted with the attention span to excel at chess, but I admire the strategy. Just like you can win a chess match in multiple different ways, you can choose to skirt fear or find ways to use it to your advantage.

Have you noticed that everyone always thinks they could be a better CEO than the CEO? Before becoming CEO when I was running various divisions of Primerica, I miraculously always knew what my superiors should have done. That's quintessential ego, right there. However, when I stepped into the role, it was a different story. New responsibilities always equal new perspectives, and with them come new anxieties.

Today, I help leaders of big companies build the relationships they need to move their people in the direction of trust so that they will act despite their fears. Without action, there is nothing. In a corporate structure, trust is often hard to establish because of fear. Leadership and team members each have their own list of doubts and worries about each other. It takes honesty and transparency to find the common ground that lets us set aside our fears.

In my role as a consultant and advisor, you might be surprised to know that while I am experienced and capable, I still have days when fear sneaks up on me. After all, I'm human. I have days when I wonder if I am doing enough. Am I making a big enough impact? Am I serving my loved ones and family while still promoting leadership and helping people become who they want to be in life? I worry that I am not sharing enough information with you, or that I am not doing enough to equip the next generation of leaders.

Then I remember there is no vaccine for fear; there is only a whisper of immunity and the dogged determination to keep going until you are proud of all you've accomplished.

3

UNCERTAINTY WEARS MANY FACES

Humans existed for millennia as cave dwellers, hunters, and gatherers. The decisions we made for eons weren't, "Should I open a coffee shop?" or "Am I really qualified to apply for that position?" They were, "Is it safe to leave the cave?" "Will I be trampled by a wooly mammoth?" "Will I be eaten by a lion?"

Our brain seeks out uncertainty in our environment so it can evaluate, plan, and prevent harm. To do so, it alerts us of the threat or uncertain outcome in a number of ways—worry, self-doubt, even people-pleasing. According to behavioral scientists, our penchant for worry is just critical planning gone awry, our self-protective skepticism always asking, "Is this the right move?"

I believe this function of our brain is well-intended. Nature, in its wisdom, wired us to instinctively mitigate risks, a survival mechanism honed through millennia. Who knows the rabbit holes we'd go down if we lacked the inclination to watch for danger? However, this self-protective instinct can take a detour into treacherous territory when we are exposed to negatively-charged environments, fierce competition, or the specter of failure.

What seems to have evolved is a combination of our natural inclination to doubt with what studies refer to as "social contagion," where behavior, emotions, or conditions spread spontaneously through a group or network. This is where the nature versus nurture debate comes in, as the world around you has an influence on what nature gave you. The result: a propensity for self-sabotage. The intersection of self-preservation and doubt, when left unexamined, can lead us down a path of hesitancy, holding us back from realizing our full potential.

One of my favorite quotes is from Henry Ford who once said, "Whether you think you can, or you think you can't—you're right." Believe it or not, the function of your brain is not to convince you that you can't. It's to ask you if it's safe to do so. This distinction is pivotal.

The self-doubt that creeps into your thoughts is not an outright denial of your abilities. When you think of it like a cautious inquiry, a primal instinct whispering, "Are you sure it's safe to embark on this journey?", self-doubt no longer sounds like an accusation.

Understanding this interplay between our evolutionary wiring and environmental influences can be empowering. You are unveiling the inner workings of your fears, exposing them not as insurmountable obstacles but as signals from a vigilant mind that is constantly assessing the landscape for potential risks. You have the opportunity to redefine your relationship with fear and recognize it not as an adversary to be defeated, but as a companion prompting you to proceed with mindful awareness.

As you turn your fears into fuel, you must unravel the layers of conditioning that have woven fear into the fabric of your thoughts. The process involves recognizing that the protective instincts of the brain, while essential, need not shackle your potential. Instead, they can serve as guiding lights, illuminating the path to growth and resilience.

THE MENTAL GYMNASTICS OF WORRY

I tend to say that a setback is a setup for a comeback. If you've ever seen a Weeble Wobble toy or a child's weighted punching bag, you know that Weebles wobble, but they don't fall down. Those punching bags, they will pop right back up and surprise you.

You can and should always get back up from any setback. The plain truth is that the setback and the comeback are two sides of the same coin. Where you find one, you will find the other, if you look for it.

Uncertainty and fear are universal. It doesn't matter who you are or how significant you might be. You will absolutely battle with uncertainty. Daily, you'll spend mental energy on uncertainty in the guise of worry. Did you turn off the stove before you left for work? Did you handle that conversation with your co-worker well? Should you have worn your blue shirt instead of the plain white one? Did you call your new love interest too soon? Did you compromise your integrity? Should you have taken that opportunity? Are you in over your head?

Every single day, almost every person you know or encounter will have a litany of things they've questioned their decision or judgment about. The only certainty in life may very well be uncertainty.

Sometimes it takes a lot of courage to sit there like a bump on a log when your mind is wildly shouting these doubts in your head. But the key to this problem is to pay attention to the language around it: *these are doubts in your head*. They are not fire ants in your pants or tiger sharks in your pool. They are just doubts, thought energy moving on through as they go drive the next person who will listen to them nuts. You might have to hear them, but you certainly don't have to take them as Gospel truth.

INSECURITY AND PEOPLE-PLEASING

I have always been a pleaser. I can't remember a time when I didn't want others to like me and wish for the people I cared about to be happy. My mother, Ruth Addison, was a pillar of our community, and everyone adored her. I was no exception. I loved my mother dearly, and the thought of disappointing her was more than enough incentive to avoid any behavior that might do just that.

I have remained similarly committed to maintaining satisfaction or happiness in other personal relationships and the workplace. Throughout my career, when challenged, I tended instantly to assume that I was in the wrong. My inner dialogue always sided with my colleague. *They are probably right*, I would think. I like to think I am humble, but I'm not that humility-filled. I was, and often still am, insecure.

I remember the first time I came across the face of uncertainty described as people-pleasing. It almost didn't make sense. Aren't children who behave well in school in the process of people-pleasing? What about the mother or father who gets up early to prepare their kid's favorite breakfast? Aren't both of those examples of people-pleasing too? I would argue that it depends on the reason or motivation behind the behavior.

Sometimes we please others out of personal insecurity, just so we can feel better about ourselves or we're hoping to manage another person's emotional state. Do you know what drives this kind of relational dynamic? That's right. Fear. This behavior comes from a desperate need to help others be okay so that you can receive their approval.

On the other hand, we might offer pleasing behavior because it is an appropriate cultural norm or a kind, loving thing to do. Do you know what you will find under the surface of the relationship dynamic between our pancake-flipping dad and his child? Love, actually. Shut your eyes and imagine what life might be like if you always acted on behalf of love and kindness. Pretty spectacular, huh?

So, yes, people-pleasing behavior can be unhealthy when it stems from a need for external validation and fear of rejection. But remember that it can also demonstrate a healthy understanding that giving and receiving are reciprocal in their very nature and is actually *good* for your relationships.

It is easy to think you are the only person struggling with doubt and uncertainty. It's very much a vicious cycle. Breaking out of this cycle requires faith in yourself. It requires you to stand firmly on the ground where you know you are enough. It truly comes down to whether you need others' approval or if your own will suffice.

Because ultimately, fear comes down to one person: you.

REFRAME THE FOCUS OF YOUR FEAR

First and foremost, fear is in the future. Unless you are falling down right this very moment as you are also somehow reading this book, whatever fear you possess is a future-you issue. That fact alone (again, unless you are simultaneously reading this book and traversing a decaying footbridge over the Amazon) should help you to pause and think when you feel afraid.

Pay close attention to the way you think about what you are fearful of. Do you tend to make statements, even to yourself, that begin with "What if I …?" such as "What if I don't finish that project?", "What if I am not smart enough to figure out that problem?", "What if I can't….?" Questions based in doubt almost always focus inward.

This is because fear is forward-facing and egocentric. Egotistical behavior is usually associated with overconfidence, I know. However, it is far more common for folks' egocentrism to be focused on their perceived fears than it is to be concerned with their perceived superpowers. I'll come back to this in a moment.

All fears tend to be an exercise in self-protection. The difference is what you are trying to protect yourself from. Fear of an external threat tends to manifest in a direction opposite that of egocentric fear. You ask questions like, "What if that noise I heard is a bear?", "What if the lack of research holds back this much-needed innovation?", or "What if a tornado touches down and stops the project?"

Notice the focus of those fears isn't on you but on the external object or challenge you're facing. Take care to understand what exactly you are trying to protect yourself from. The next time you catch yourself behaving poorly or you notice another person's poor behavior, ask yourself, what am I (or they) afraid of?

When you clearly understand what you are afraid of, you can shine a light on it. You can reframe the fear and begin to make rational choices based on an actual challenge rather than the egotistical fear you might have created.

You can also acknowledge that your fear is in the future. This perspective makes it much easier to take back a position of power. As you sort through worry and anxiety attached to an outcome that hasn't even happened yet, you can discard ideas that have little merit and prepare for the scenarios that do seem possible. Without this reframing, fear can twist and turn into anger and other emotions that further confuse the real issue.

The next thing you need to do is to tell your inner critic to stop discouraging you and to start *en*couraging you. I've found that positive self-talk doesn't come easily for most people, myself included. You need to consciously train your inner voice to stop saying, "Oh, you screwed up. You should have done this instead." That kind of thinking will leave you mired in the quicksand of fear and doubt. Instead, speak to yourself with words of hope, courage, and compassion. Remind yourself of all your positive traits and unique superpowers. I know you have them and I bet, deep down, you know it too.

Back when I was at Primerica, encouraging and inspiring our sales force was baked into how we did business. We wanted our people to see themselves the way that we saw them: as talented, driven, brave, and worthwhile. Heck, we *needed* them to believe in themselves in order to successfully weather the storms we went through as a company.

I recall one particular event where everyone received a shower hanger card. Printed on the cards were morning affirmations: *I'm a great person. I'm a great recruiter. Today, I will meet the right people in the right places for the betterment of all.* I thought that was a brilliant idea—you get in the shower and, next to your bar of soap and shampoo, you see these positive words that remind you to feel good about yourself. As you wash your body, you get a little "brain washing" as well.

Learn to discern whether your fear is ego-driven or stems from an external threat, remind yourself not to worry so much about something that hasn't happened yet, and train your inner voice to say, "I've got this." These are all useful tools in the quest to build confidence and overcome uncertainty and I recommend you use them. But to really stop fear in its tracks, we have to go deeper.

LOOK FOR THE SOURCE OF YOUR FEAR

If you are insecure and full of doubt, where does that come from? Can you pinpoint it? If you can, you have the ability to disarm it simply by looking at it. However, you will have to look at it very closely and with even more self-honesty than you might think you have. Courage is what you'll need, but I have good news for you. If you can act with courage, you are already moving through fear.

Winston Churchill was always trying to impress his father. This desire created fear and uncertainty in his life. Interestingly, that same desire allowed him to fuel the actions that led to his success. He had a mission that was bigger than himself, a reason to get involved in politics. He didn't know he would soon be saving the free world, but he felt the weight of his destiny calling to him, and so he marched on, allowing his fear to fuel his actions.

To discover where your fear comes from, you'll have to ask yourself some hard questions, such as:

- Do you have friends with a frequently negative perspective?
- Did your parents have heavy expectations of you?
- Have past failures or missteps caused you to be insecure?
- Have you lived in the shadow of a successful sibling, friend, or parent?

I can't answer these questions for you, but I can promise you that if you consider them carefully, you might find some of the external reasons you doubt yourself. Just like you can't rewire your brain in an instant, you won't be able to immediately separate from events or circumstances that shaped how you respond to decisions and opportunities.

You can think of your newfound awareness like getting a new bicycle when you're used to walking everywhere. You'll have to learn to ride it, but once you do, it'll help you get where you are going more quickly.

THE BRITISH BULLDOG

In May of 1915, Winston Churchill found himself demoted from First Lord of the Admiralty of the British Navy to a cabinet post so obscure it is rarely ever noted. (Chancellor of the Duchy of Lancaster, if you're curious. If you are further curious about what the heck a Duchy is, it's a dukedom or the territory of a duke or duchess.)

Why was he demoted? If you remember your world history lessons, the Dardanelles Naval Campaign and the Battle of Gallipoli may ring a bell. History papers are still written today both in support of and focusing blame on Churchill for the military landing plans that resulted in a bloody stalemate and the loss of forty-six thousand allied troops during World War I. Newspapers shouted out in big, bold headlines that Churchill's days in politics were over. Though he was absolutely shouldered with and burdened by blame, he very literally soldiered on.

Churchill woefully admitted to a friend that he believed he was finished as a leader, but he did not hide from the fight. In November of 1915, Churchill resigned from the government and took up arms. He took a direct route to the front lines in France. His new title? Infantry officer—a far cry from admiral.

After facing near death on the battlefield, Churchill rejoined politics in 1917 when he was appointed minister of munitions. Still, it would be years later before the whole world would know the name Winston Churchill. His ability to convert his own fears and insecurities into fuel for his next step has always been an inspiration to me.

USE UNCERTAINTY AS A TOOL

All decisions come with some doubt. It is a tool to help you judge the safety and the reality of a situation and to perhaps explore alternative options. In this way, there is a positive power to having doubt. Having too much certainty limits our ability to be open-minded and receptive to other perspectives. It leads to the opposite of tolerance and makes us blind to the world around us. If you do not have a little bit of insecurity—or what we might call healthy skepticism—you are prone to act like a bull in a china shop.

However, we must take care not to conflate healthy doubt with our self-worth. Remember: skepticism is useful, but self-sabotage is not. Use doubt to determine if the robocall is a scam (it is). Engage doubt when buying a car. On the other hand, give doubt the boot when it comes to your ability to act on an idea. Don't let it paralyze you into inaction. Even if you choose not to act, you are still making a choice.

In life, with any important decision you make, you are going to have doubts. You can't know for certain if it's going to work out. You are not going to know what the results are ahead of time. None of us are blessed with that ability, despite what someone from the Psychic Hotline might tell you. You'll never have that perfect piece of information that tells you when and how to act. But if you think things through and do your homework, you *can* act on your ideas consistently and with a degree of confidence. Even if your decisions don't make everybody happy and even if things don't work out perfectly and you start second-guessing yourself, you can trust that you made the best decision with the information at hand. I know, because I believe in you.

That said, I don't mean you should plow forward with reckless abandon. It's always good to temper forward motion with some rationality and discernment.

The careful balance of conflict and confidence is what you have to keep in mind. Think of a set of scales and visualize times in which conflict and confidence absolutely outweigh one another. An everyday example might be the conflict you could feel when presented with an opportunity to partner with someone on a business deal. If you're being asked to do more or contribute more than your counterpart, the scale might tip on the side of caution, and it should. You would need to ask more questions and understand the expectations better before you commit.

Now think of a time you feel you may have missed an opportunity because you were too cautious and gave in to the voice of uncertainty. What about a time when you feel you won because you took a risk? If you can envision those scales and try to keep them somewhat balanced, you'll find yourself in good company.

Many of the best leaders and some of the most successful people in the world, were bold but humble. They knew what they knew and, more importantly, they recognized what they *didn't* know, they learned from their mistakes, and they worked with others to achieve their goals.

Whatever it is you desire to do, you can likely learn enough to pull it off. Whatever you don't have the natural ability to do, you can probably find someone to do it for you.

Think of goals like you might think of remodeling your kitchen. You can probably manage to paint the walls yourself. You might even watch a YouTube video and successfully replace the faucet. You wouldn't give up on replacing it if you couldn't do it yourself, though. You'd call a plumber. Business goals work a lot like this, as do personal goals such as fitness or weight loss. Do all you can do on your own. Learn all you can to be as effective as possible, and then partner with someone who can help you the rest of the way. There's no need to wallow in self-doubt because you don't have the talent or knowledge to tile your backsplash. Just recognize when you're uncertain and out of your depth and then ask for help.

It is okay to get help along the way. In fact, I highly recommend using mentors and advisors. Do a little digging, and you will find that most of the top income earners in the United States credit a mentor, an advisor, or a partner with their success.

And, should you find yourself in a situation where you seem to be going backward, just remember that Churchill went from admiral to infantry before he saved the world. Setbacks will occur, and they will usually contain a lesson that will create a better result in the long run.

4

COURAGE IS NOT COMFORTABLE

"Courage is the first of human qualities because it is the quality that guarantees all others."
~ Winston Churchill

We tend to associate courage with bravery and heroism. These concepts can certainly be related, but the courage I am talking about doesn't involve swordplay or slaying dragons. (Honestly, sometimes it takes far more courage *not* to fight. Violence is easy, which is why it's prevalent.)

The word *courage* has an interesting etymology. The Latin root *cor*, meaning "heart," gave way to the French word, *corage*. You might already know that's where our word comes from, but what is often overlooked is that second syllable, which is from the Latin word *agere*, meaning "to lead." Put the two together, and you discover that to have courage means to lead with one's heart. Maybe this is why Churchill said that courage is the quality that guarantees all others.

It sounds nice, but leading with your heart is not for sissies.

We know that courage and fear are not mutually exclusive. In fact, courage requires by definition that you act in spite of your fear.

Fear is often incredibly persuasive, so much so that it is a tactic of war and torture. Ideals that inspire fear can paralyze and confine entire populations. Yet, courage in the face of fear shatters the façade and has, time and time again, changed the course of humanity.

Courage, the kind that changes the fate of nations, institutions, belief systems, and ideals, is most fortified when it is inspired by the heart and leads us to a greater sense of purpose. We go outside of ourselves on behalf of something bigger. Think of soldiers who sacrifice themselves on behalf of a nation they love. Without that love and loyalty in the back of their minds, they are just people meeting their fate in the field. But in the context of service, leadership, and love for their country and what it stands for, they become symbols or extensions of the ideals of the nation itself.

Willfulness isn't what does that. Courage does.

Odds are, you are not charged with freeing the masses from oppression and your quest is much less dire. Still, taking action in the moments you need to do so can feel exceptionally daunting.

DECIDE WHERE YOU ARE GOING

Most acts of courage are *not* heroic, at least not in today's idea of what heroic means. Hopefully, you avoid the need to run into burning buildings or leap them in a single bound.

The courage you most often muster may not require that your life be in peril, but I doubt you'll find it a cakewalk either. Employing courage is not comfortable, my friend. It is, instead, convicting. It's the small voice that tells you that conformity is a form of cowardice. It is the inner impetus for action. More often than not, when you act with courage, you are the contrarian in the story. You're pushing the proverbial envelope. You're defending the innocent. You're going up against old ideas that no longer serve anyone. You're working to inspire change that feels right and good.

None of that is ever easy. In fact, it can be downright terrifying to walk that path. You must find courage in your convictions.

Art Williams is known for saying life will give you what you fight for. He also says—maybe more importantly—*life will give you what you are willing to accept.* He is absolutely right. I don't think we have to duke it out for everything we desire in life, but persistence is crucial. Our society is full of people who quit when things get hard. You might be astounded to know how many people have stopped thinking about what they actually want and are now just floating through life with little direction.

To get where we want to go in life, we must be willing to fight, to persist, and to get after it. "Okay, John," I hear you saying. "I'm ready to fight. But where do I start?"

The concept of knowing where you are going in order to get there is pretty simple: You need a destination to chart a course. Your destination is your goal, and the course you take should be informed by what you hope to learn and experience on the way, as well as what you are able to be, have, and do when you arrive.

Setting goals, voicing your desires, and creating intention all set the path for a life well-lived. In order to achieve the outcomes we hope for, we must learn to make choices that stay in line with the principles of that path.

It's when life smacks up against our beliefs or our values, or impacts our progress, that our courage falters and we tend to lie down and quit. The other option is to stand up, speak out, and act. Sometimes we are forced to do this in the face of danger. But most times, opportunities for courage are far more subtle. There are times when courage could even be considered mundane.

Stay with me here.

I want you to think about your achievements in life, both great and small. Would you consider your achievements the product of work or luck? Anything we feel we have achieved, we generally would agree that we have worked, trained, or practiced to make happen. In order to make things happen, we have to implement the systems and habits to make them possible and keep going on our chosen path.

There is courage in sticking to your path to realize your goals.

An athlete trains, eats well, and tries to ensure they sleep well. They learn the art of visualization and the power of positive thinking. These habits set them apart from the masses. There is courage in getting up thirty minutes early to prepare yourself for the day. There is courage in choosing to sleep rather than watching television. There is courage in making a tough choice over an easy one. An overnight success story that is actually true is about as mythical as a unicorn. It's the courage to put in the work that paves the way for change and, ultimately, for success.

TAKE STOCK

Do you have a big, bold, exciting goal for your life? Do you journal about it? Have you made a plan with steps to get you there? Have you thought about life once you hit that goal?

Before we go any further, let's take stock of where you are.

Start by setting a goal, one you feel you can reasonably achieve. I feel reasonably confident you can accomplish any goal you set and work for (you're taking action by reading this book, right?), but you have to believe that, too.

Let's start with something uncomplicated.

How about the ten thousand-steps-a-day goal?

What can you do that would get you closer to achieving this goal? Would thinking about how and when you can fit more steps into your day help? Perhaps. After all, there's nothing wrong with being intentional. But I'd wager the more effective tactic would be just to get moving.

I am not sure why the simple acts of getting up, putting on your shoes, and going for a walk seem so much more daunting than writing a detailed plan for how to fit one thousand more steps into your day, but I know it can feel that way.

In my experience, the key to tactical thinking and subsequent action is being realistic about what you can do, what you will stick to, and what will work for you. That's why small, daily action is so effective. Lots of people set long-term goals. But the reality is, there is no long-term success without short-term victories.

Erk Russell, three-time national champion head football coach at Georgia Southern and longtime defensive coordinator at the University of Georgia, would tell his players all the time, *It's another day in which to excel.* I think that's exactly right. We have to view every day as a day to get better, a day to move forward. Now, that doesn't necessarily mean we're going to be successful every day. Some days won't turn out the way we want, and some days we're going to screw up. But guess what? We can get up the next morning and get better from there.

That's how you need to do life: Get up, and get after it.

Back to our ten thousand-steps-a-day challenge and what it takes to get it done.

If you can start hitting ten thousand steps a day right off the bat, man, I am envious. For reasons beyond my knowledge, some of us are built to get out of bed in the morning and hit the ground running, and some of us are not. I can honestly say, I don't ever look at a treadmill and think to myself, *My God, I can't wait to get on that thing.* Some of us need to find a reason beyond "it's good for me" to really get moving. Now that I'm retired and am not constantly on the go because of work, my reason has become my dog, Winston.

When we're vacationing in the mountains or at the beach in Florida, Winston and I walk and walk until we're both tired. I get in twelve-to-fifteen thousand steps, easily, and don't even realize I'm doing it. We both enjoy those walks tremendously. He gets to run and sniff things and explore, while I get the joy of watching him have fun and the satisfaction of knowing that I'm taking good care of him. The fact that I am also achieving my daily goal of ten thousand steps and taking care of myself is almost incidental.

The plain truth is, we don't always feel that internal drive to do the things that need doing, especially if those things are tough, overwhelming, or scary. I think this is especially true when the goal we're trying to reach is one we've set for ourselves—after all, who's going to know if we don't get out and walk today? In the hubbub of everyday life, it's easy to make excuses and let ourselves get distracted.

To get motivated and stay that way, you need to think of a reason that really matters to you. Maybe your motivation is to stay healthy for your kids. Maybe it's because you enjoy spending time with your friend and walking partner. Or, maybe it's so you can be ready for bathing suit season. Whatever your reason is, keep it front and center in your mind and commit to doing what it takes to get the job done.

Let's think of a little more ambitious goal.

What if you want to make an extra five thousand dollars each month?

Deciding how you'll make the money, what you'll sell, or what services you'll offer are the strategic parts of the plan. But we're learning to approach and engage in tactical thinking, so what might all of that look like in more detail? What are the small-scale actions you can take to get yourself to your goal?

Life moves on the smallest of decisions. For example, regardless of how you plan to make this extra money, there aren't any more hours in the day. Do you need to get up earlier? Do you need to study a craft, or do you need to earn some credentials? Do you need to find a mentor and schedule time with them? Do you need to clear some clutter out of your extra bedroom to create a workspace? Do you need to sell the unused golf clubs in the garage for seed money to get started?

Likely, the steps are even smaller than those mentioned. Are you getting enough sleep? Are you eating well? Are you moving your body? How well you take care of yourself matters. Minding your thoughts—that matters even more.

So what can you do right now? If you lay this book down, what can you do, small as it may seem, to get yourself closer to your goal?

Maybe you need something as simple as a glass of water and a healthy snack. Or, maybe some gratitude is in order. No step can be considered too small if it advances your position. You can take one small step at any time, and then you can take one more small step, and so on. And you know what? All those steps add up fast.

There is no magic sauce here; you'll have to figure out where you must grow, learn, and evolve. Chances are, you know this already, so now you just have to decide what actions you'll take.

GET YOUR REAR IN GEAR

You can write down your goal and even a detailed plan to reach it; but that goal isn't real unless you do the daily work necessary to achieve it. Until you take regular, focused action, your goal is only a pipedream or a wish. This is why it is crucial to establish habits and systems that will help us to succeed along the path.

Unfortunately, as humans, we tend to lose focus and go astray, and end up with habits that hinder our progress. I am no psychologist, so I won't attempt to diagnose you or the lot of humanity. However, I will say I have been around the block a time or two, and I've made some observations that have proven to be accurate.

When we form bad habits, there is usually something in our psyche that pushes us to this form of self-sabotage where we avoid the good habits that could help us succeed. When people self-sabotage, often it's because they do not feel they can succeed, or they don't feel worthy, or sometimes, they feel like an imposter in their own lives.

If you feel this way, let me offer you some reassurance: Unless you're in the witness protection program or practicing dentistry without a license, you are probably not an imposter.

The best way I've found to combat that insidious voice that tells us we're not enough, is to establish a pattern of continued growth. Set a goal, plan a course of action, then act. At the end of the day, ask yourself, *Did I move a step closer to my goal today?* If not, vow to try again tomorrow. It is through our consistent, repetitive actions—better known as habits—that we can silence our internal inner critic, achieve incremental growth, and write the story of our future.

One of the best habits I've formed over the years is diligently focusing on being in a *state of becoming*. Doctors have residencies, elite athletes train daily, and former CEOs of publicly traded companies—they read and continue learning to stay connected and relevant. As I said at the beginning of this book, we are all human *becomings*.

We'll talk more about habits later in this chapter. For now, I'll just say this: If you've ever tried to establish or change a habit, or create the systems you need to achieve a goal, then you already know it is not a comfortable process. The truth is, the amount of time and unseen effort between setting a goal and achieving it is rarely exciting and can be filled with intermittent fear.

During this phase, we are up against a fear of failure and a desire to conform. We fear we will expend our effort without achieving a tangible result, completely missing any small wins along the way. Also, we fear that if we go against the norm, and we expend our effort without recompense, we will look foolish to all the other people who don't bother to take those chances in the first place.

Some people even go so far as to convince themselves that it's better to have no goal at all than to have a goal, develop a system to attain it, and then fall short.

Why do people do this?

Over time, the best answer I've come up with is, people who are determined to have absolutely zero goals in life do so because that's the one goal they are guaranteed to achieve. It's like these folks are in a boat without a rudder, letting the winds and waves of life carry them along because that's easier than using the oars sitting at their feet. These also tend to be the ones who are most critical of others who dare to try. I'm guessing you know a few people like this.

They say, "Who do you think you are to swing for the fences?" They do not want you to succeed, because, if you swing and hit that triple, what might that say about *them*? They, too, could set goals, put in the effort, and make big moves. But they haven't. Are they lazy? Failures? Cowards? That's the underlying fear behind their eyes when they look at you: If they see you succeed, how will they feel by comparison?

(Try not to be too offended by these folks. If you have ever measured yourself against someone who seemingly outshines you, then you know, it's not a fulfilling feeling.)

Of course, the worst critic you'll ever have to face is yourself. Fear almost always plays a supporting role in our self-criticism; we get very afraid of our own judgment and will do anything we can to drown it out. The limiting beliefs and fear of failure are right there outside the door, along with those hoping to witness your fall. Under these circumstances, the courage to act can be hard to muster.

This is the time to summon your inner advocate (he or she is there; if you knock, they will answer, I promise). When you catch yourself putting off a decision or action out of fear, it's crucial to take stock of your thoughts to recognize the difference between a legitimate reason for your hesitation and self-sabotage.

Why is this so important? Because flipping back and forth between action and indecision is a killer of dreams. It is exhausting and painful, and that is the very opposite of what I want for you.

Here's a thought: What if you just laid down that self-critical, fearful mantle? What if you didn't morph in and out of those roles of being motivated and working one moment and being your very own internal hater the next? What if you ignored the hater in your head? What if you told the hater it was flat-out wrong and just got down to work instead?

CHASE THE HABITS

It's ultimately our habits and the practices we put in place that help us to achieve the results we hope for. Determination, sacrifice, and drive make the difference. Consequently, it's not determination in the face of success, it's our determination in the face of failure that moves the needle.

It is important to understand that the great achievers in the world did not just randomly hit their goals. They got where they wanted to go by creating systems and habits. Failure was frequently their path, but they *failed well*—they adjusted their aim, and they made those failures actually mean something. They found great purpose in their flops. The failures informed how they chose to proceed, and that is everything when it comes to overcoming obstacles.

Listen, goals change. But creating systems to achieve outcomes, those are enduring. Getting good at the systems and habits and being adaptable enough to tweak the habits and systems is the key to meaningful change.

What are these habits and systems?

They can vary based on what you're trying to achieve. For example, if you're trying to go to the Olympics for swimming, you'll need some non-negotiable athletic prowess. But no matter what your goal is, you have to understand and practice the following principles:

1. Combine hard work with consistency to achieve true success. People are generally in favor of hard work, but we are less good with consistency. Let's just use the example of a New Year's resolution to shed some pounds. You might show up that first week and work your tail off. You're sore. You're tired. You start thinking about the coming weeks, months, and maybe even years. How long could one person possibly keep this up? You start to favor rest, relaxation, and maybe you even call it self-care. Your hard work felt transformative, but you have let your consistency dwindle. (You are human, after all.) To turn those initial results into true success, you've got to show up to work hard on a regular basis.

2. Prioritize your personal happiness. Even in the midst of a big, hairy, audacious goal, if you are not taking time to smell the roses, you will burn out, and there goes your consistency. This might seem to contradict the first point above. It's about balance, not pushing yourself to the brink of insanity or even injury. Find the thing that reminds you of why you are reaching for that big goal in the first place (remember my pal Winston?). Visualize the happiness you'll feel as a result. Prioritizing that? Now, that's called inspiration.

3. Roadblocks are inevitable. Be ready to adjust course. Resolve is the name of the game on the road to success. When you are fretting about how to overcome that roadblock that feels like it's going to halt your dreams, it's important to take a step back to see what's really happening. Is your goal still attainable if you can get past this thing standing in your way? Or, has reality shifted such that what you were hoping to achieve is no longer even the right goal?

If it's the former, then resolve to go over, under, or around whatever is standing in your way. If it's the latter, you may need to rethink your goal and chart a new path. Try not to be discouraged! Life throws us curveballs sometimes. The key is to keep moving, even if it's in a different direction than we originally expected.

4. *You may be your biggest roadblock, so work on yourself.* Investigate what motivates you, what inspires you, and what drains you, so you can respond to any given challenge instead of reacting poorly to it. You can learn to circumvent certain negative mental processes simply by watching them. You might see your tendency to do the self-sabotaging thing. In the beginning, you may very well indulge in that. But after a while, you'll start to recognize the pattern, and then you can insert some rationality into the mental process and chart a course of action to avoid your regular pitfalls.

5. *You're not that big of a deal; don't take yourself so seriously.* Beware, false humility is a real thing. It's hard to learn how to be authentically humble. You have to act yourself into a new way of being. Practice regular humility. Even if it goes against your self-concept or propensities—even if you feel like the biggest imposter on the planet—if you begin to embody the principles of humility, one day you will sit up in bed and realize that you have actually become that way. You can't take yourself so seriously that there's no room for adjustments, new ideas, or full pivots. A humble person can admit when the plan is not a viable one, when they need to ask for help, or when they need to adjust the loftiness of their beloved goals. A humble person knows that there is greatness in being ordinary.

As for the right habits to get you to your goals, you have to determine the ones that serve you best. I can tell you to get up early, to journal in the morning, to meditate under a tree, to exercise, or to sit in a hot sauna until you see springtime, but I cannot know with any certainty if any of that will help you.

It helps many people to get up early and to begin the day with a small win. It also helps many people to go for a walk. Those things will probably help you as well, but the best advice I can give you is to emulate the habits of a person who has achieved the same or similar goals as the ones you've set for yourself. You have to find a person who has what you want (either figuratively or literally) and then make similar, effective moves.

Whether you want to make a gajillion dollars trading cryptocurrency or if you're trying to break the world record for balloon animal making, I'm not going to pretend I know what specific systems you need to put in place. Study those who have gone before you, but don't assume their habits or systems are perfect. Inject your own personality into the actions you need to take, and then aim and adjust.

SHOOT FOR THE MOON

The heroes of my youth were not movie stars or rock and roll legends. They were astronauts. I was born in the late '50s, right around the time the Space Race was in its infancy. I was approaching three years old when John F. Kennedy charged Congress with putting a man on the moon.

The next few years were exciting for us as a nation. For me, they were unequivocally formative, and they sparked my imagination. There was just something about those men who were brave enough to float around in space that made me feel like anything was possible. As a little boy, I had no clue what it would actually take to perform a moonwalk. Though advancements in space technology and aeronautics dominated the news cycle, to be an astronaut was a far-flung concept.

So how did people achieve this position? The first astronauts were military test pilots, individuals who were already elite in the field of aviation. They were mavericks who'd already defied gravity. Those vying for a chance to go to the moon endured grueling testing and training. From pressure chambers simulating an altitude of sixty-five thousand feet to high-heat exposure and countless other mental stability tests, eventually seven men stood out—the Mercury Seven. Can you imagine the perseverance it took to be chosen from more than five hundred elite pilots?

What habits and systems did these men have in place long before the Space Race was announced? These pilots were literally the best of the best of the best. Did they employ positive self-talk? Did they surround themselves with like-minded ambitious people? Did they learn that pivoting does not mean failure, it just means finding a different way? My guess is *yes* to all of the above.

As a small child, I had no grasp of what the Mercury Seven went through even to be qualified to volunteer to be part of history. Later, I would learn that Admiral Alan B. Shepard, Jr., the first man the United States launched into space, was a tremendous human being. Shepard was a farm boy who worked odd jobs as a teen at the local airfield to learn about airplanes. He was an excellent student. Though the entirety of his education was obtained in a one-room schoolhouse in rural New Hampshire, he won an appointment to the United States Naval Academy. After serving on the destroyer U.S.S. *Cogswell* in the Pacific during World War II, Shepherd trained to be a pilot and went on to the U.S. Naval Test Pilot School in Patuxent River, Maryland. He flew experimental planes such as the F3H Demon and the F5D Skylancer and served as an instructor at the school. He also attended the Naval War College.

He accomplished all of this *before* he became an astronaut. The following quote speaks volumes about Shepard's outlook and perspective on life:

"I think, first of all, you have to be there for the right reason. You have to be there not for fame and glory and recognition and being a page in a history book, but you have to be there because you believe that your talent and ability can be applied effectively."

For me, it's the last bit of that quote that resonates: "...you believe that your talent and ability can be applied effectively." Whatever it is that you are hoping to accomplish, do you feel the same as Shepard did about his role as an astronaut? Do you believe that you can apply your talent and ability effectively? If so, what in the world is stopping you? Shepard and his counterparts went to the *moon*! Shepard went from a farm to the moon.

Let that sink in.

What habits and systems did Shepard, John Glenn, Gus Grissom, Scott Carpenter, or any of the test pilots who volunteered for Project Mercury put into place that allowed them to succeed at that elite level? How did they adapt to the demands on their bodies and time, the risk to their lives, and their privacy forever altered? You've probably seen those clips of zero gravity simulations and stress tests, but the astronauts had to have the mindset to deal with all the challenges of their fame, the danger they would be in, the impact on their families, not to mention learning to eat nothing but freeze-dried food! Getting to the position that puts you in a seat on a rocket to the moon took uncommon dedication, resolve, an open mind, and the ability to adapt.

(Incidentally, I don't know if you picked up this book because you are trying to get a job at SpaceX so you, too, can go to the moon. If you are, I hope it helps.)

I feel like most of us can really win at life with only a modicum of the effort the Mercury Seven employed. These were men who were top aviators at a time when aviation was a relatively new technology. How did they get to be so brave? What pushed them forward? As a rule, we can achieve notable success with far less bravery and tenacity.

John Glenn was awarded six Distinguished Flying Crosses and eighteen Air Medals during his career as a Marine fighter pilot. After that, maybe making the first transcontinental supersonic flight was a piece of cake, but I doubt it.

One of my favorite quotes from John Glenn is, "I'm not

interested in my legacy. I made up a word: 'live-acy'. I'm more interested in living."

Dare I say that all astronauts have a bias for action? They are interested in applying their talent and ability where needed and living each moment to the fullest. I believe we can take notes on that and inspire our own action, our own courage, and our own live-acy!

5

TACTICAL THINKING

If you haven't guessed by now, the very best way that I know to turn your fears into fuel is to get out of your head and act. The more you stew in your thoughts, the harder it is to get your rear in gear.

"That sounds great, John," you say. "But where do I start?"

You start by learning the difference between procrastination, planning, and execution. You learn to think tactically.

The word "tactical" generally relates to military endeavors, but it can also mean small-scale actions that serve a larger purpose. Strategic thinking, on the other hand, is the overall plan to achieve your goal. Tactical thinking is determining the daily incremental actions that get you closer to the goal. When you think tactically, you ask questions like: What do I need to do today to move forward in life? What can I do today to get closer to my goal?

People have big plans, but big plans require big effort. Big effort requires getting up every day and choosing to do the things that move you further along the path. This is a daily battle—a tactical battle.

As my career has evolved over the years, from running a large company to being an advisor, consultant, and board member, I've often run into companies that focus on their future in the name of strategy. Executives sit in meetings pondering what they want the company to be in twenty years. They understand their purpose and the legacy they want to build. However, without spending the same amount of energy building short-term plans to reach those long-term goals, I assure you, they won't happen.

While I understand the value of the bigger picture, I believe there is even more value in seeing the everyday for what it is: real opportunity. No one should get so caught up in what will happen in the next ten or twenty years that they fail to live the days they are given. My advice for people who suffer from chronic forward thinking is to perform where your feet are. Understand where you stand and how that position helps you today. What can you do to maximize your opportunity now? What actions can you take today that will benefit you today?

If you're ever worried about the past, present, and future all at the same time, always choose to focus on the present. The past doesn't exist anymore, and the future has yet to come. Right now is the only thing we have to utilize. Everything else is just inspiration for our actions.

CAST YOUR LINE

Recently, I went trout fishing, and I caught a four-and-a-half-pound rainbow trout—a whopper! Naturally, I was very excited, and I posted a photo of my catch on social media for my friends to see. The comments ranged from congratulations to good-natured jealousy and some excuses for why a few folks hadn't been fishing in a long time.

I thought the range of comments was like a micro-study of human behavior. Some saw my catch as an inspiration and used it to plan their own fishing adventure. Others were envious and didn't feel they could do what I had done, and the reasons for that belief ran the gamut. I was luckier, more skilled, had more time, had better equipment, and on and on and on. I don't know how many times I have cast a line for a fish in my life only to reel in an empty hook. I do know this: If I hadn't cast the line, I wouldn't have caught anything.

It is easy to watch others on social media and get envious of their life, looks, hobbies, money, and fishing prowess. But what you need to remember is everything you see on social media is carefully curated to appear a certain way. People don't often show their bad days (well, some do *only* that, but that's for another time). Most of those people who are doing things you might envy, are doing so because they have likely done them in the past. It is not their first time ice skating when they show you a triple axel. What you don't see are the hours, years, and perhaps even decades that go into each moment of success. You can't look at the finished product and think that was a one-off success. They likely had a plan, a course of action, took steps, suffered setbacks, and then tried again.

In chapter four we talked about the discomfort that comes with finding the courage to set goals and act on them. Fear will tell you that you do not have what it takes to endure all the failures in between the start and the major success, but that's just plain untrue. How do I know? Because if it were true, no one would ever accomplish anything. So, you have to think tactically. How can you get from point A to point Z in small increments that are feasible? What can you do today to get started taking a step in the direction you want to go? What can you do today to get a little closer to your ultimate goal of landing that big fish?

FIVE DAILY ACTIONS TO GET YOU STARTED

Like I mentioned, you will be the best judge of the habits necessary to move you forward. However, there are a few daily actions you can take to be better at sundown than sunup. I have found over the years that these five approaches to life make the journey much easier and more enjoyable.

1. BE HAPPY

Happiness is a choice. You must choose to be happy. For every single smiling face I see in an airport, I see ten frowning faces.

If you don't make an absolute choice to be a positive, upbeat, happy person, you probably will not be. Any of us can find a million reasons to feel crappy today. Making a conscious decision to look for the positive, be positive, and exude that positivity, that's a meaningful action toward a successful life.

Life is short, don't waste it being miserable. Happiness comes from the heart, not just the smile you wear on your face. All of the time, I hear people say, "When these bills are paid off, life will be better," or, "When I find my husband or wife, then I'll know true happiness." Life's circumstances are conditional, but your outlook on this world doesn't have to be. Happiness is an inside job. Period. There are no two ways about it.

Stay in the moment you are in and appreciate the now. I promise, the arrival of money, love, fame, or whatever you think is the one thing that will make you happy is rarely the thing that brings true happiness. Happiness that relies on circumstances to be perfect or ideal is, at best, fleeting. At worst, it's an illusion. To stay happy, choose happiness now, and then in the next moment, and the next.

Years ago, at the church Loveanne and I were attending in Snellville, Georgia, the pastor said something that still runs through my head today. He said, "If you want to be happy, if you want to feel better, sometimes you have to program your brain to think that way. Act the way you want to feel, and soon you'll feel the way you act."

Act the way you want to feel, and soon you'll feel the way you act.

I'm not advocating for burying your negative feelings deep inside, never to see the light of day. If you have continual and pervasive negative thoughts that haunt you, they need to be faced and moved through, just like your fears. But there is a truth to what that pastor said. Sometimes it takes a little bit of a fake-it-'til-you-make-it attitude to achieve a positive mindset. When I find myself feeling a bit down, making the decision to carry myself as a happy person translates to feeling genuinely happy. Give it a try.

We can all agree that challenging circumstances will arise from time to time; that is just a fact of life. However, happiness is a conscious decision, and you control your decisions. Circumstances can make for a rough day, a tense week, and sometimes a season of growth. To grow in your positivity, you have to find the good. When the good is hard to find, grace is a substitute that will allow you to surrender to what you cannot control and make way for peace. In peace, there is solace.

Gratitude is another excellent stand-in for what is good. When we are grateful, we aren't focusing on what is wrong. We can see the everyday mundane as a gift, which is exactly what it is. Not one single day is promised to us, so when the good is as elusive as a raccoon who's found a way into your pantry at night, try practicing gratitude. You'll notice a difference.

This isn't just lip service. Science supports the power of positive thinking. I am proof of this. In my book, *Real Leadership*, I recall the details of my stroke and my recovery. This was a dark time. I was scared to death. I'd never had anything remotely serious happen to me health-wise before.

Nietzsche said, "He who fights with monsters might take care lest he thereby become a monster. And if you gaze for long into an abyss, the abyss gazes also into you."

Let me tell you, there is no greater abyss than realizing your mortality with full force. When death gazes back, and you decide to give up, you sign your warrant. I have great hope that you are not battling a major health crisis and don't need to stare down the reaper and tell him to back the hell up.

There is a particular scene in the movie *A Beautiful Mind* when the main character is sitting for tea and is told he has been nominated for the Nobel Prize. As he's discussing his life and his experience with schizophrenia, he mentions that even after all this time and all he's accomplished, he still often comes face-to-face with his personal demons manifesting as hallucinations. While that once made him fearful, he explains how he makes an active choice now not to acknowledge them, saying, "I choose not to indulge certain appetites." That's a powerful statement.

While most of us are not battling schizophrenia, there is quite a lesson to be learned from Russell Crowe's character. We all face things in life we don't expect, things that make us uncomfortable, and we have thoughts that muddy our minds and bring us down. To that, I have always said, "Feed your dreams, starve your nightmares." While it can be hard to face our negative thinking, we can find comfort in knowing our thoughts are just thoughts. It is important we attempt to reroute our way of thinking when we find ourselves indulging in the thoughts that hold us back, make us feel bad, and tell us we aren't enough.

Your attitude determines so much more than you realize. I was determined to heal from my stroke and thrive and continue my life with even more passion and vigor than I previously held. I made a complete recovery.

I'll go ahead and tell on myself because it will make Loveanne chuckle when she reads this. My doctor told me I had a child-like brain. He meant relative to my brain's ability to heal and create new neural pathways, but my lovely bride would beg to differ and offer up many examples to support her own conclusions about why that statement is true. Either way, you can get your information from James Allen's historical text, *As a Man Thinketh,* or you can get it from *Brain and Life Magazine,* but both explain that positive thinking is good for you. Researchers at

Johns Hopkins University think it has something to do with reducing the inflammatory damage of stress. One hundred years ago, James Allen said, "As he thinks, so he is; as he continues to think, so he remains."

It's pretty clear that choosing positive and happy thoughts is the best option.

2. DON'T COUNT ON SHORTCUTS

With enough time, tenacity, and effort, there's not a lot in the world that you can't make happen. However, progress for most people is a "three steps forward, two steps back" daily slog. Remember: Big plans mean big effort.

Most of us can't skip to the head of the line. Most of us do not win the lottery. Most of us do not have the ability to easily lose thirty pounds. Most of us achieve what we do inch by inch. We succeed because we are committed to the small, daily actions that beget success. While that's a hard realization—that there's no magic bullet, secret hack, or hidden door to achieving your goals—it's also pretty great to learn that you don't have to go on an odyssey to obtain a magic bullet, learn a secret hack, or find a hidden door. You just need to take consistent action.

The University of Georgia football team won the National Championship in January of 2022. (By the way, they won it the next year also.) I would argue that they did not win on the day that they won the game against Alabama. Rather, they won in countless daily practices when they were running the stadium stairs. They won in each and every moment when they improved their strength and stamina. They won each time they focused on their mental aptitude to do so. They won with consistency and perseverance. They won in the lessons they learned from the previous year's losses. They won because they believed they would. That's no shortcut.

While I used the word "slog" above, which means a long,

laborious walk, you must remember that tremendous effort does not necessarily equal misery. You can delight and revel in your journey just as easily as you can find total displeasure in it. Life is that way, remember? Happiness is an inside job. You can see the stairs to your goal rising long and tall before you as an endless climb requiring toil and painful exertion; or, you can see those same stairs as a golden bridge to transcendence, as an opportunity you might not otherwise have, one you need only seize upon to move yourself forward.

Now, to be blunt: Opportunities are for the fortunate. Not everyone in the world has the luxury of being able to focus on their goals. They are too busy trying to survive—finding clean drinking water for their families, navigating disease and economic depression, or avoiding war-torn areas in an effort to save their own lives. The fact that you have the *option* to choose to see the goal in front of you as a slog or a golden opportunity is not only a gift, it's a perspective that is entirely up to you.

3. MANAGE PROCRASTINATION

Learning to manage procrastination is a huge stepping stone when it comes to hitting any goal.

Years ago, when I was young in business, I worked with someone who would hand out funny awards. If you were someone with a propensity for saying, "I'll get around to it", he would give you a big wooden circle that had 'A ROUND TUIT' burned into it. It was a joke, but the message was clear: Do what you say you are going to do. People fall into the *someday* camp or they find themselves in the land of *As-Soon-As*, and they get stuck there. As-Soon-As Land is a purgatory where dreams go to die.

Somewhere along the way, we started to believe that procrastination equaled laziness or a lack of self-control, but this just isn't true. Behavioral science tells us that procrastination is an emotion regulation issue.

Usually born of boredom, insecurity, self-doubt, resentment, or anxiety, procrastination is a method of coping with fear. Once in a while, it can be task-related. Honestly, who really enjoys cleaning the toilet? Yet, much more often, you're locked up in a negative emotion about the task. You could be worried you can't do it well. You could be angry that you have to do it because it's not your job. Or, you could be suffering from overwhelming feelings and are not able to mentally chart your way to your destination with any clarity. You don't know where to start. If any of this resonates with you, I would encourage you to ask yourself, "*Why am I avoiding this task?*" Naming the negative emotion you're feeling and facing it is the first step to overcoming it.

I originally titled this tip "avoid procrastination," but you and I both know it's not that simple. You can't just tell yourself to stop procrastinating. Even after you've identified the root cause, you still have to figure out how to make the reward for completing your task better than your go-to guilty pleasure when you're avoiding the things you know you need to do.

There are some ways to manage procrastination. Let's use the example of cleaning the bathroom. It's a dirty job. Perhaps you feel totally overwhelmed just at the first thought of having to clean it. Maybe it makes you feel clammy and like you're going to gag. Maybe you have a true physical aversion to it. If you can't mentally commit to cleaning the whole bathroom, could you commit to one task within the bigger goal, like cleaning the sink? You can do that, right? The sink isn't that bad at all. And, once that sink is sparkling, you can quit right then and there, leaving the dirtier, dingier parts for later. Congratulations, you now have a manageable plan for action.

You gather all your cleaning supplies. You spray, start wiping, and you can see the change immediately. The clean surface gives you a renewed sense of purpose, even if only for this brief moment. You become a cleaner of sinks. As you step back and see this sparkling wonder, you think, *I could probably keep going and wipe down the countertop*. You find some satisfaction in how easy it is to take care of the countertop. Then you see the toilet. You have to clean it now. How could you not? Before you know it, the bathroom is clean. *You* just did that! Even when you didn't think you could.

It worked because you gave yourself permission to not complete the entire task. You only committed to one small move. You removed the mental pressure, which created space for your ability and motivation to come flooding in. All you had to do was take one step in the direction you wanted to go. Then you found some momentum. At that point, it didn't make sense *not* to keep going; you had to. Anything else would just be porcelain-based insanity.

Do you see how getting over the initial hump of procrastination can turn into a job well done? All you had to do was take one small step for man and leave that giant leap for mankind in the background until it was ready to take hold of you and finish the job itself.

Remember: you may delay, but time will not. Don't let your dreams litter the ground of As-Soon-As Land. There is a lot of clutter there already. (Not to mention, the bathrooms need cleaning.)

4. ATTACK THE DAY

As I write this on a Sunday evening, I imagine people are dreading that tomorrow is Monday. The weekend is over, and it's back to work. They are not happy. Watch out—I'm here to tell you that negativity and unhappiness are contagious. If you're feeling sad the weekend is over when you show up to work on Monday morning, then you're at your desk out of obligation and not at your best. That may seem harsh, but anything less is not the truth.

Carpe diem, or "seize the day," is an ancient expression. One of my favorite football coaches in the world, University of Georgia's Kirby Smart, regularly encourages others to "attack the day." Personally, I often say to myself and to those who come to hear my speeches, "I will do today what others don't, so I will have tomorrow what others won't."

What it boils down to is this: Make the most of the time you are given. Don't start tomorrow or next week. Start today. Start this very instant. Use the time you have to do *all* you can to the best of your ability, and try to be happy and excited to do it.

I understand. It's hard to want to seize anything except your pillow when you're tired. The rigors of this world don't often allow us the rest we need when we need it. Sometimes the work we have to do is not the work that inspires us. I understand that your life is not perfect, and you have challenges that I am not aware of. I, too, have dealt with difficult coworkers, unfair supervisors, spilled coffee, missed lunches, and traffic jams, and I've had my hopes dashed. I have been in the trenches with a shovel, and I have absolutely had very bad days. You're not going to get through life without the messes. What I have learned is, no matter what adversity we are dealt, (so far) the sun still rises the next morning. You can choose to wallow in the challenges, or you can choose to try and rise above them. You can choose self-pity, overthinking, and paralysis, or you can put one foot in front of the other, smile at passersby and do your best to have the best day you can have.

Sometimes, having the best day you can simply means getting up, feeding yourself, and brushing your teeth instead of staying in bed with your head under the covers. That is okay!

Progress, when we've been dealt a heavy blow, looks different for everyone. All I can advise is to aim for progress, even if it's micro-movements in a positive direction. Try not to squander your time; it is more of a luxury than you might realize.

On good days, begin with the idea that you get to make a positive impact on the people around you. You get to accomplish a set of tasks. You get to collaborate with your co-workers. You get to make someone laugh or smile. You get to try to make the best of the time you have before the sun sets and you lay down to rest.

Attack the day first by appreciating that you have a day in which to move the needle of your dreams closer to fruition. Beyond that, I hope you use each day to help others see their talents and find their purpose in the world.

5. ALLOW YOURSELF SOME GRACE

Life moves on the smallest of decisions. Sometimes, those decisions aren't always the right ones. In those moments when you realize that you've zigged when you needed to zag, you have to forgive yourself, find the lesson in the experience, and move the heck on.

This entire book is about learning how to use your fears to motivate you toward success. Well, one of the most common fears I've encountered is a fear of screwing up. None of us wants to look stupid or incompetent. But here's the thing (and I know you've heard it before, but it bears repeating): Every person I have ever met has made a mistake. Every. Single. One. I promise you that every person you have ever met has also made a mistake. There's no evidence to support that you are the only person in the world who has screwed up. So you're off the hook. You can cross this fear off your list.

It's funny, we tend to be quite good at forgiving others. Yet we are not so great at granting forgiveness to ourselves. Allowing yourself some grace in the moments when you mess up is important to your success. If you stay mired in your mistakes, whether they are big or small, you stay stuck. Guess what you can't do if you are stuck? You cannot work toward small, consistent actions that will get you where you want to go. If you can forgive others when they mess up, surely you can give yourself a mulligan.

As you work toward finding those small, daily actions you need to take to advance in life, I hope you'll form some new tactical habits.

I hope you'll develop a bias for action, even if it seems like the action is insignificant. I encourage you to develop the habit of choosing to be happy and positive as much as you possibly can. As you start to recognize when you've crossed over the line from planning to procrastination, I hope you'll ask yourself why you're avoiding the task at hand. Then, remember to develop a habit of self-reward for getting things done. Learn to appreciate the opportunity in each brand new day and allow yourself some grace when you stumble while learning and practicing tactical thinking. After all, like the proverb says, to err is human, to forgive divine.

6

THE ART OF GRATITUDE

In this technological day and age, the reminder to practice gratitude is everywhere. Open any social media platform and next to the ranting and raving about everything that is wrong, you'll see boatloads of gratitude memes, messages, and heaps of blogs about gratitude. But being grateful is not a post on the internet. Being grateful is not a meme. It's a way of life. So what does it mean to live a life of gratitude?

Gratitude is one of the most, if not *the* most, fundamental ingredients for a happy life. So what does it look like to experience gratitude? When was the last time you were truly grateful for something or someone? What about being grateful for a stumble? Is that even possible? That would be even more challenging than being grateful for the good things.

You can't just curate your online persona to appear grateful and leave it at that. Well, you can, but if you want to see lasting change, if you want to experience all the growth and transformation that life has to offer, you will have to expend some effort. It's not useful to just look at and share memes in the hopes that something will change. As leaders, we have to do introspective work and then take the outer steps to follow it up. Otherwise, nothing—and I mean nothing—will ever change.

In the spirit of doing introspective work, you can set the tone for living a focused and happy life by making a daily list of things for which you are truly grateful. Some people keep a journal and write about what they are grateful for whenever positive things come up. Others choose to make one long list and check back with it regularly. Still, others choose to make a list of things they are grateful for each and every morning. It's your list, and for that matter, it's your gratitude, so you can feel free to make it what it needs to be for you. The trick is to make it something you revisit regularly so that those positive feelings of gratitude really sink in and become something you can call upon when you are having a bad day.

A DIET I RECOMMEND

Scientific studies have proven that gratitude is a healing emotion. It has been shown to reduce stress levels and free up the brain's reward pathways, which allows chemicals like serotonin, oxytocin, dopamine, and endorphins (all the happy chemicals we generally cheer on) to get where they are going. That means you experience more satisfaction in your day-to-day life. Isn't that what we all want?

The feeling of gratitude has also been proven to lower heart rate and reduce the occurrence of everyday aches and pains as it helps to lessen inflammation. In addition, gratitude increases oxygen flow within the bloodstream and supports appropriate and healthy immune responses. Heck, it even helps balance your sleep-wake cycles, allowing you to feel refreshed after less sleep! I am grateful for what my gratitude diet has done for me, and I recommend you give it a try.

OLD-SCHOOL GRATITUDE

Anyone can say they are grateful for anything at any point in time. What makes gratitude powerful is not merely scribbling it down in a notebook before you rush out the door to your next meeting or to get the kids off to school; it's actually getting out there and practicing it.

The power of gratitude is the inner feeling (and outer circumstances) you cultivate when you are grateful for something. If you aren't sure what gratitude should feel like, I often compare it to a feeling of love and peace that go together. Think about something or someone you love and then contemplate the loss of that. You don't need to consider the loss for very long. If you got a sharp pang, a few beads of sweat, a sinking feeling, or even some tears, you're in the right place. But now consider that you haven't lost anything or anyone, thank goodness. For me, gratitude is what remains when I realize that I still have what I love in my life. Gratitude is what I feel when I actively appreciate something or someone.

I was fortunate to have Guy Clark, who was a great American songwriter, play at my 50th birthday party. He wrote a song called "Old Friends" that perfectly expresses how I feel when I think of my loved ones. Here are some of the lyrics:

> *Old friends, they shine like diamonds.*
> *Old friends, you can always call.*
> *Old friends, Lord you can't buy 'em.*
> *You know it's old friends after all.*

When I think of my family and my old friends, I feel a sense of peace and ease knowing they are there for me. When I bring each of them to mind, when I envision their smiling faces and can "feel" them in the room with me, love and appreciation lights me up. I feel gratitude for each one of them and what they have brought to my life. For me, gratitude is more about that very palpable feeling than it is just ticking a box or sharing a meme saying I am grateful for something. I want it to be real, because if it's not, I am the one who doesn't get to experience the dividends that being grateful pays.

I said that gratitude is what I feel when I realize that I have something in my life, but I want to be crystal clear about what I mean. It is possible to be grateful for things we have lost, as well—my mom, for example, rest her beautiful soul. I am grateful to have had her in my life. I am grateful she set me on the path she did when she suggested I marry Loveanne (not that I didn't already plan on doing it). I had my mom's blessing, and I am forever grateful for that. I am grateful for the lessons she taught me about treating people the way I wanted to be treated and about stepping up and taking the lead when leadership was necessary.

My parents and the good company they kept taught me so much that still informs who I am to this very day, and thank goodness for that. Recently I had the pleasure of attending a service to celebrate the 200th anniversary of the church we attended when I was a youngster. As I sat in the pew, I thought about all of the wonderful people of that congregation who played a pivotal role in my development as a person.

These were not wealthy people in any material sense; but, boy, were they wealthy in spirit and goodness. They were hospitable and caring for others, showed up for their community when needed, and made sure others knew they were appreciated, especially during difficult times. Values such as these were passed down from generation to generation. These upbeat, positive people that I had the pleasure of spending so many Sundays with showed me the power of being grateful for what you have.

In fact, witnessing the way these folks went about life taught me the true meaning of success. Real, honest-to-goodness success looks like happiness. It means that in the scarce time you have on this mortal coil, you are fundamentally happy—you wake up most days feeling good, feeling positive, feeling happy. It has absolutely zero to do with money and everything to do with your ability to feel gratitude and your decision to choose happiness.

If you are someone who thinks money will solve all your problems, please trust me when I tell you that it absolutely will not. If you don't believe me, consider this: Money is a multiplier. It can help a fundamentally happy person to be even happier. But if a bad or fundamentally negative person comes into money, all that does is give him an excuse and a means to spread his negativity. Either way, it has little to do with true success.

So while I miss the days of breaking bread with those incredible role models from my youth, I will always cherish the lessons they taught me. I am so profoundly grateful for the wisdom they imparted to me. And while I don't get to see my mama's sweet Georgia smile anymore, I still carry the love she demonstrated to me and the appreciation she gifted to others. The gratitude *she* was raised with lives on in that way.

GRATEFUL FOR TOUGH TIMES

Are you feeling the gratitude yet? Are you feeling the warmth and love and happiness that true gratitude offers? If not, you might want to go back and re-read the last few pages to fortify yourself. It's time to address the hard stuff and you may not like what I have to say.

Life is not easy, y'all. I get it. The world is crazy. In twenty years from now, the world will still be crazy. We can complain about the times we live in, but guess what? Unless you have a time machine, you're stuck here with the rest of us. When you notice yourself getting caught up in the negative and scary news of the day, stop and remember that the best way you can make the world better and more positive is for *you* to be better and more positive. Influence people not by what you say or post on your social media feed, but by how you act and who you are. Choose to be a light in the darkness.

Let's go a step further.

What if there was a way to actually be grateful for the challenges and craziness all around us? What if we embrace it? I know, I know. Hear me out.

One of my all-time favorite movies is *The Outlaw Josey Wales*. (If you haven't seen it, I highly recommend sitting down with some popcorn and preparing yourself for something great.)

There is a scene where Josey's character, played by Clint Eastwood, is trying to empower the other pioneers and settlers with whom he has traveled, worked, and lived. Their lives and livelihood are being threatened. The people are scared. Taking a position of leadership, Josey pipes up and says, "Now remember: When things look bad and it looks like you're not gonna make it, then you gotta get mean—I mean plum mad-dog mean. 'Cause if you lose your head and give up, then you neither live nor win. That's just the way it is."

In life, it's not enough to endure adversity; you have to embrace it. You have to embrace it to get through to where you want to go, and sometimes that means getting "plum mad-dog mean."

One of the things that I have trained myself to do—yes, this takes training—is to always seek the lesson in the struggle. *What about this trial can I be grateful for?* This is not an easy question to ask; it requires great courage and the willingness to accept that, despite the negative, there is a positive in there somewhere, even if you have to plumb the depths or go digging. If you look hard enough, with enough honesty, I promise, you'll find it.

Sometimes the positive or the lesson isn't immediately visible to us. I know you've heard the idiom hindsight is twenty-twenty. I can't count the number of times I failed to see a single positive aspect in something for a good long while. I really struggle sometimes. But when I have some distance between me and the circumstance, with the situation clearly in the rearview, I can recognize there is always something to be grateful for, especially in our challenges.

Knowing what does not work is often as valuable as knowing what does. If you have experienced a failure in life, a loss, or a challenge that didn't go your way, when viewed through the proper lens you'll see you now have something extremely valuable: information. Information is the foundation for future choices and actions; it helps inform how we move in the world. What could be more valuable than that?

When we set aside the emotionality of a loss or failure, we can see that losses, trials, challenges, and failures are what give us the opportunity to be great. Without them, we would just float around living a life that is only partially informed about what it takes to succeed. I don't know about you, but a win after a setback—when I've been able to adjust and re-aim—is so much sweeter than win after win after win.

When Rick Williams and I were in the middle of negotiating Primerica's exit from Citigroup, there was a time when everything came crashing down. All the countless hours of hard work went entirely down the tubes. It was as though the life was sucked right out of us. We had been defeated, punched in the gut, and were struggling to see the silver lining. I was so down and out, I wasn't sure there was any blue in the sky behind all of the clouds.

I was afraid. I thought, *even if we do get the opportunity to go through all this hard work again, what if it still doesn't amount to anything? Is it worth it?* Honestly, I wanted to give up. I seriously considered giving up.

Then I remembered why I was doing what I was doing. I envisioned the faces of all the people who helped make Primerica the successful company that it was. I pictured the families attached to each one of those faces, the children, the elders, the people who directly supported those people, and then I recommitted, and I dug in to try again. Rick and I had discovered what didn't work, so this time, we would try again and investigate a different avenue. In the end, we wouldn't have succeeded in the way we did without that initial failure. With my twenty-twenty hindsight, I wondered, *Was it actually a failure? Or a success in the making?*

There are few days as memorable as that day on Wall Street when Primerica went public and the cheers erupted. There were smiles for miles as we celebrated our shares going up and up. And that's what they did for the rest of the day—they went up and up and up!

At one point, right after we were on television to celebrate the announcement of the IPO, I looked at Rick and this thought flashed through my mind: *I almost gave all of this up because I was afraid to try again.* I had almost let fear win. We had almost lost the fight. I had almost walked away. Can you believe that? I shudder to think of the damage that might have ensued had I chosen to give up at that point in time. I almost let fear stop me from reaching my destiny, and—for that matter—helping Primerica realize its own destiny.

A swelling of gratitude entered my heart, not only for the success of the company, but also for what that success would mean for all of the people who fought alongside us. Once again, I thought about all of the loved ones who depend on and support our Primerica family—and while I was already on cloud nine, I could not wait to celebrate our collective success together. Let me tell you, a shared achievement is *infinitely* more rewarding and fulfilling than an individual one.

That win was so sweet because of the trials we endured as a team to get to it. If it had been easy, would it have felt as worthwhile? After all, it's the struggles that make you strong. When you learn to be grateful for the struggles, you know you are making great headway as a leader.

Sit with that for a minute: The struggles are what make you strong.

No one said this was easy, but it sure is worth it to take a minute and reevaluate how you approach your life's circumstances in your mind.

The win might have been worth it for everyone else; and yes, that would have been more than enough. But what it did for me, for my faith in God and my faith in my ability to keep going even when I thought I couldn't possibly take one more step, that experience forged a new paradigm at my core. It solidified my understanding that, even in the worst of times, I must always be grateful for the learning, shaping, and struggles that are taking place.

GIVING IT AWAY

I once met a guy at a conference who sat down with me afterward to talk about some of our shared experiences and views. He intrigued me. He had lived a life almost completely opposite to mine, but as we spoke, I felt like I needed to know whatever it was that he knew. He was inspiring. I was in the presence of real leadership.

At one point during our conversation, he said something that made me pause and think. He said, "You can only keep what you have by giving it away." I had to consider it for a while, even after he explained. He wasn't talking about things or objects; he was talking about legitimate, living spiritual principles. This reminded me very much of a quote widely attributed to Winston Churchill: "You make a living by what you get; you make a life by what you give."

I want you to think of someone you know who seems to have more joy than you could ever fathom having at once. Everywhere they go, they grace their company with their presence and a smile. Good energy radiates around them. Heck, even the lightning bugs want to follow them around at night to get a taste of their light.

Now imagine someone who's always negative. A real Eyeore-type character. Nothing ever works out for them. Nothing is ever worth trying because it always goes badly. No one appreciates or understands them. They don't believe they will ever get a chance to make a difference; even if they did, it probably wouldn't matter anyway. They wander the halls of life in an existential crisis, telling anyone who will listen about their woes.

For reasons I cannot fathom, it seems to be an unwritten rule in life that the Eyeore folks will share their feelings at a much higher rate (and more loudly) than positive people. If you lead an organization of two hundred employees and ten of them are negative, I guarantee you will hear so much more from the Eyeores than from all the others combined. That's because happy people generally don't go around telling people they are happy; they let their attitude and actions speak for themselves. Everywhere they go, they spread joy because that is what they are filled with and their lives are richer for it.

On the other hand, Eyeore gets to keep his sadness and his doubt because that is all he has to give away. This person is almost inevitably lonely because, while misery loves company, even misery has a breaking point at which it has to run for the hills to save itself.

Now ask yourself: *What kind of person am I?* Be honest. If you find yourself identifying more closely with Eyeore, the good news is, you're self-aware which means you can change if you want to. You can make a conscious effort to share some happiness and gratitude.

I'm a bit of an old-school guy, but one of the more New Age principles that I think is spot on is the law of attraction. When I am happy, when I am not so concerned with helping myself as I am helping others, when I am more focused on shining my light on others or my team, that is when I find myself most fulfilled. And isn't fulfillment what we all really want to experience anyway? I find myself surrounded by purpose and support when that is what I offer to others. Isn't that odd? While it might be sort of odd in the world of Newtonian physics, in the Quantum Realm, it's reality.

I find that I am most grateful when I share that gratitude with others. I tell them how grateful I am for their service, give them a smile, or write someone a note to express my gratitude for who they are and what they do for me or someone else. In other words, I get to keep my gratitude because I try to constantly give it away, and that's what keeps it coming right back to me.

Gratitude is an essential element in the antidote to fear. Fear is based in the future, remember, while gratitude is grounded in the present moment. When you choose gratitude, you choose the present, and the present is a place where fear has no foothold.

We can absolutely learn more from what goes wrong than from what goes right, and we can use those lessons to help cultivate gratitude in difficult times, even when we are afraid. Without the setbacks that shake us up every now and then, if life is always smooth sailing, it's easy to get complacent and drift off course. Do not let the small wins along the way lull you into thinking your work is done. That's how success ultimately becomes its own worst enemy.

Real success isn't a moment or a season; it can be the way you live your whole life. You can't let adversity and challenges get you backed into a corner. You have to become grateful for them and then transform them into success. It's exactly what Josey Wales said: If you lose your head and give up, then you neither live nor win.

A REGULAR PRACTICE

I will admit, a state of gratitude isn't natural for most people. Like anything worth doing, it is something you have to work for, train for, and strive toward. As a leader, shying away from the tough work on ourselves doesn't inspire others to do their own tough work. We want to lead by way of service to others, to shine our light, and a regular gratitude practice is one of the very best ways to accomplish that kind of leadership.

I mentioned some methods for bringing more gratitude into your daily life earlier in this chapter, but if you are still struggling, you might consider developing some mindfulness to ease your efforts. Consider this: If you are grateful, it means you are not resentful. Resentment drags us down like an anchor pulling through a mud bog. So how do you stop resentment from killing your gratitude? You have to nip it in the bud. Don't bite the hook of resentment. You might be the big rainbow trout expecting to get a juicy meal, when all you get is hooked and yanked right out of the water.

When I first started practicing mindfulness, I had to learn to observe myself quite a bit. Right at the moment I would start to feel resentment, I would ask myself, "Why do you feel this way?" Usually it was because I felt like I was right and someone else was wrong, or because something in the world should be other than it was. But did I really know I was right, or did I just think I was right? Right according to whom? Was this a position I was getting hung up on? Usually it was.

When it comes to feeling resentful for something out in the world just being the way it is, I like to use the analogy of the old man who stands outside and shouts at the clouds just for being in the sky. Now, why would anyone do that? I'll tell you why: it's because we are human. We all have a secret stake in how things go, how our lives unfold, and how life treats us. The harsh reality is that this is all a mental fabrication. When I find myself cursing traffic, I have to remind myself to let it go. Those little irritations, those tiny rubs we experience throughout the day, those are the ones that hook us and kill our opportunity for gratitude.

So when I say gratitude takes practice, I mean actively evaluate how you approach obstacles in life. Are you willing to let resentments keep you from your full potential for success and a happy life that awaits you in the grateful present moment? Are you going to let your anger and the fear that underlies it paralyze your possibilities?

At the end of the day, our fear can either suck us dry as we drain everyone around us; or, we can utilize that fear as a reminder to ourselves that we can be grateful for challenges, growth, and pain, and use it as fuel to pave the way for meaningful transformation.

I've said it before, and I'll say it again: If it's meant to be, it's up to me. Well, you. But you know what I mean. You are the only one in charge of how this all unfolds. Gratitude springs from within, but when you choose to give it away, you keep that positive fountain flowing. That is how you bolster the people around you, how you help fortify and build others up. When you build others up, you can't help but rise to the same level.

Gratitude really is the gift that keeps on giving. It ensures that you stay in the present moment, which is the only place where potential meets action to become success. So, what can you be grateful for today that you never even considered being grateful for before?

7

COMMIT TO THE JOURNEY

ROCKY ROAD

Mountain ranges: gorgeous to look at—not easy to navigate.

Way back when, just after I graduated with my undergraduate degree, my great friend David Croom and I took a trip along the West Coast in the summertime. We were driving across the country with our windows down and not a care in the world as we approached the expansive and beautiful Rocky Mountains.

If you haven't spent much time in the mountains, I will tell you this: they are not all created equally. The Blue Ridge Mountains are beautiful, and I love spending time around them when the leaves change, but the Rockies are a whole other ball game. You can just keep driving into them, and the next mountain always seems bigger than the one you just passed. Today, I think God built the Rockies to help give us perspective. However, at the time of our trip, little did I know that a mishap would provide me with just that.

David and I were heading into the Collegiate Peaks area of Colorado where our plan was to experience as much nature as we could. With all of our camping and fishing gear, plus food and backpacks and clothes, my 1973 black-and-red Maverick was busting at the seams with everything two guys needed for a cross-country adventure. On this particular day, we wanted to find a place to camp in the back country, away from the main road. Our goal was to make it to a certain lake along the tree line. We would hike in, pitch our tent, and find a place to go fly-fishing.

Now, you have to remember, back in the technological dark ages known as 1979, GPS did not exist, nor did cell phones. We began our drive up the mountain armed with a giant U.S. atlas and some national forest maps we had picked up from the park ranger's office. I was driving and David was navigating. At first, everything was great. We were oohing and ahhing every time the road curved and another stunning view was before us. After a while though, the road started getting rough. Then it got rougher. I started to think, *this doesn't look right.* By now, we were ten thousand feet up, on a dirt road with cliffs and boulders on either side of us. Needless to say, it was very treacherous.

"David?" I asked, glancing over to the map in his hands and trying to make sense of the situation. "Are you sure we're on the right road?"

That's when we realized: The line on the map David had been following was not a road but a river. (At least, that's *my* recollection. David would undoubtedly tell you the real problem was that I hadn't followed his directions.) The little Maverick, David, and I were jumping and bumping on what we later learned was a U.S. Forest Service fire road.

We were lost. Now we had to make a decision. We had half a tank of gas. Was it better to turn around and try to retrace our route, or just keep going?

I won't lie—I was scared. I was afraid we had gone too far up the wrong path. By that point, we had made a bunch of turns and I wasn't sure if we could find our way safely back down the mountain. With the path narrowing and boulders jutting into the trail from every side, I wasn't certain we could turn around even if we wanted to. To make matters even worse, it had started to snow ... even though it was August. I knew we weren't going to freeze to death—we both had appropriate coats and gear—but even so, seeing that white stuff coming down didn't do much to calm our nerves.

Unsure of what to do, part of me (the part that was catastrophizing and contemplating all of the horrible possible outcomes of this situation) thought we should just find a good spot to camp until someone came along to save us. Hopefully that would happen before the next spring thaw. *But who does that?* Who just gets lost or delayed and decides to make camp in the wilderness and call it a day? Looking back on this situation, I realize that many people do this. Many people who feel lost in life make their camp in the lost place. They set up shop, create relationships, and take jobs, ultimately treading water for decades in the lost place. They become content with simply surviving.

As it turns out, David and I weren't quite ready to throw in the towel. We kept driving until we came upon a wide, flat outcropping facing west, just as the sun was about to set. And wouldn't you know? There was someone there camping.

Talk about a deep sigh of relief! I am not a big fan of asking directions, but you can bet your boots that I asked that man. He told us if we kept going in the same direction, in fifteen miles or so we'd hit the main road and be back in the town of Salida. He also suggested that, first, we should camp for the night. After hours of white-knuckle driving filled with uncertainty, that sounded pretty good to us. We proceeded to enjoy an unbelievably gorgeous sunset together, and the following morning David and I made our way back to civilization.

It might be an exaggeration to say that kind man saved our lives (though he did likely save us from running out of gas in the middle of the Colorado wilderness). But when we finally turned off that bumpy road and onto the highway the next morning, I sent up a silent prayer of gratitude nonetheless. *Thanks for getting us out of that one safely.*

Later, in 1993, Loveanne and I decided to take a family vacation in Colorado. My sons, Tyler and Kyle, were five and eight years old. We rented a Jeep and had a wonderful time exploring the Rockies together.

On one of our drives, we came across the very road that led to my and David's misadventure all those years ago. Only this time, rather than spending the journey in fear and uncertainty, I drove with confidence along that bumpy, twisty-turny road. We went back to the exact same spot where David and I had met our unlikely guide and, together, Lovanne, the boys, and I camped for the night. To this day, we all enjoy reminiscing about that experience.

What started back in 1979 as a true journey into the unknown has become a core, lifetime memory for my family. Thank goodness David mistook that river for a road, and thank goodness we pressed on, even though we had no idea what lay ahead.

GET OUT OF THE TUB

If you haven't already guessed, getting lost on the high trails of Colorado would turn into a metaphor for getting lost on the high trails of life. Typically, when we get lost on the road, we *do* something. We check the GPS. We check a map or (God forbid) we ask for directions. So why, in other areas of life, is fear enough to get us to stay put?

Winston Churchill said, "I never worry about action, but only about inaction." Inaction is as detrimental to our growth as anything else. In fact, it's probably *more* detrimental. After all, if you resign yourself to inaction, hoping to stay safe and comfortable in that warm bathtub of fear and complacency, then it is one hundred percent certain that you will grow into nothing except a wrinkled up prune. That water won't stay warm forever. Sooner or later, it's going to cool down, and you're going to get chilly and more and more uncomfortable until you're forced to get out. Now, you're cold, wet, and miserable, and that thing you were avoiding all along is still right there waiting for you anyway. Why wait until you're at this point?

Now, I am all for people taking baths. I like folks to be clean. But choosing to remain in that bathtub of fear because you are afraid of what new outfit you might have to put on is downright ridiculous. I know that sounds silly, but it really is that simple: Making a new life for oneself, opening up new doors, or starting new relationships often requires us to change our clothes. We might have to put on a new uniform or decide to put on something nice for a date with a new love interest.

That new outfit symbolizes the unknown. It's fresh and clean, and it might be expensive and attractive, but is it going to be as comfortable as the old favorites you sit around the house in? Probably not. We have to find a place within ourselves that is willing to take a chance and forge ahead, despite the potential discomfort of a new belt that's too stiff or a dress that's a bit bolder than your favorite pair of sweatpants.

I once took a psychology class in which the teacher made this same point with a bleak but clear example. She had a picture of a child, five years old, who was being held by a law enforcement official as they were removing him from his mother's custody. The little one was in tears, filthy, screaming, and inconsolable, reaching an outstretched hand for Mom. The mother was at the other edge of the image, being taken away in handcuffs. She was being arrested for and charged with child abuse. She had seven children, all of them having suffered terrible, untold abuse at her hands. But this little one wanted his momma, no matter how much she had hurt him. He was more afraid of moving into the unknown than he was remaining in the tragedy that was all he'd ever known.

My point is, it starts early, this fear of the unknown. It is buried within us, somewhere down in that child's brain. Fear of the unknown, and especially fear of success, is a real thing that will shape our reality for the worse if we let it. Fear of success will stop us from achieving any of our goals. It will keep us frozen in the space-time continuum as an organism that refuses to evolve, despite every opportunity in this modern world to do so. You have to consciously address these fears, refuse or refute them, and keep going. With kindness, you need to assure your five-year-old self that it's okay to move forward, that you've got this. Because you do.

Now. Are you ready to go beyond just getting out of the water and putting on clean clothes? Good. You look fantastic. Now grab your umbrella before you head outside because it looks like rain. You wouldn't think of cancelling your date because of a little rain, right? After all, you found the courage to ask them out and you've waited all week for tonight. Great, you've made it your car. Uh oh, you've got a flat tire. Now what? Time to climb back in the tub?

I think you can guess where I'm going with this.

You will not reach your goals and dreams without encountering adversity along the way. No matter how much you plan and prepare, challenges both big and small will still find you and cause you discomfort and uncertainty—that's just how life works. To truly grow and move forward, you must learn to embrace adversity. If you want to graduate from what I like to call the University of Adversity, it's not enough to simply endure adversity. *You must embrace it.*

Looking back on my career, I can see where I faced hard circumstances and had to make certain difficult decisions in order to make things happen. But I'm okay with that. Because when things are humming along just fine, it's easy to get complacent. It's the adversity that makes winners change and adjust and do the things they need to do in order to win. So embrace what's hard, wrap your arms around the difficulty, smile at it, and go forward.

FOCUSED ACTION

If you haven't noticed, I am a big fan of action. Action, focused action in particular, kills fear. There's so much dread and uncertainty in the moments before you do a thing that's causing you stress. You may need to make some phone calls that have got you feeling a little nervous; instead, you sit in worried agitation, rearranging your pen holder. The longer you rearrange, the longer you stay inactive, and the bigger your anxiety grows. As simple as it sounds, if you learn to pick up the phone and make the hardest call first, the rest will be as easy as peach pie.

The above scenario exemplifies Newton's first law of motion which talks about inertia. In case you need a refresher, this law says that objects at rest remain at rest and objects in motion remain in motion unless acted upon by an external. In my life, this has applied to both people and objects alike.

If you are stagnant out of fear (back to that proverbial bathtub), it's almost impossible to move. However, if you never stop moving, if you are always rolling in the direction of progress, it becomes nearly impossible to stop you. Which scenario do you think yields more fruit in a leadership or business setting?

By "rolling in the direction of progress," I don't mean you do things just to do them. You don't want to be that octopus on roller skates, a whirr of activity in every direction; instead, you want to be focused, methodical, and justified in everything you apply yourself toward. You have to ask yourself, are you serving another person or your team by doing what you are doing? Are you taking care of necessary tasks that require someone to check them off? Are you taking steps toward a specific goal, or are you simply afraid of sitting still (sometimes, this *is* the necessary action)? If you are afraid of sitting still, are you filling your time with action that is equivalent to procrastination?

Considering your *why*—your motivation behind your actions—will help you decide if you are taking focused action or if you are simply too afraid to sit still, hoping some of the nervous energy will dissipate in time for you to do something special. If you think of rearranging your pen holder versus reaching out to folks who might be willing to donate to your annual fundraiser, that should be a difference that is easy to discern. One action advances your purpose or your cause, creating more opportunities in growth areas. The other just annoys your overused writing utensils.

By taking action and making moves, you will find the path you are supposed to be on. Your goals will become clear.

All I can talk about is what worked for me. Was I always a shining example of flawless potential? Absolutely not. Was I always clear on what I was doing and where I was going? Nope. Sometimes I took the wrong action, made the wrong choice, and I had to back up. But only through action and activity will you find your right path. You are never going to think your way to success. You have to act your way to success.

THE WAY TO THE TOP

Popular Sufi scholar and poet from the thirteenth century Rumi said, "As you walk on the way, the way appears."

Being lost along the way is part of the journey. If you never feel lost, confused, or like you aren't where you want to be, you probably have some other super-human characteristics like magnetism or the ability to see through walls that you might want to share with the rest of us. That's not me.

When Loveanne told me she was pregnant with our first son, I was thrilled to death, but I was scared. Would I be able to do enough to take care of my wife and child? Was I in the career I would be in for my whole life? Would I need to consider something different that paid more to care for a growing family?

I asked myself lots of questions back then, but I knew that I didn't have to have all the answers to do well. I already had the opportunity, and that opportunity is what I chose to keep focusing on. With my job, I had the opportunity to learn, grow, hone my communication skills, hone my leadership skills, explore how I functioned as part of a team in a way that was beneficial to others, and I had the opportunity to be of service to folks in general. All of those opportunities are ones that I chose to act on, and those choices propelled me to a position of importance within the company.

I have come to realize that the destination itself is not the key to success. Instead, the essential factors are not only dedicating yourself to the journey but journeying well. If you commit to navigating it well, life's winding path can lead you to unexpected places with abundant potential for a brighter future beyond what you could have imagined. Just as Rumi said, as you walk along the path of life, the path itself unfolds before you.

8

A BIAS FOR ACTION

A BENEFICIAL BIAS

Merriam-Webster defines the noun form of bias as "an inclination of temperament or outlook." When I use the word "bias," I want you to think of it as an inclination or trend. If you are inclined to act, you have a bias for action. Some of us are fortunate enough to be born with this inclination; others have to spend some time cultivating it. If you are one of the latter, don't get discouraged—it's easier than you think. Just by picking up this book, you are demonstrating a bias for action.

When I meet people in a professional capacity, I will often ask them if they foresaw their current reality for themselves. I will ask something like, "Did thirteen-year-old You know this was going to happen?"

More often than not, the answer is, "No." Now, some exceptions can be made. For example, most veterinarians I meet have known what they wanted since early childhood. They love animals, and they have loved them their whole lives. But most folks I've polled with this question had no idea that their present reality would look like it does, myself included.

So, how *did* I get to the head of the table at Primerica if I did not see myself there from the beginning? A lot goes into answering that question, but having a bias for action is one of the key components.

When I returned from my trip out West in the fall of 1979, I was living with my parents and spent most of my days going to Atlanta to apply for jobs. I had no great plan; I would see a tall building with a logo on it, go in, and ask for the Personnel Department. My only goal was to get a job that allowed me to move out of my parents' house and get a place with my buddies.

The company that finally offered me a job was an insurance company called Life of Georgia. My title was Underwriter Trainee, which meant I would sit at a desk and review applications for life insurance. I'd review people's medical information and rate their applications for acceptance or denial based on their health profile.

Guess what? "Addison" starts with A.D.D., and, true to my name, I am not good at sitting, staring at documents, or doing repetitive work. In fact, I'm horrible at it. You could not have found a worse job for me if you tried. I'd watch the guys on scaffolding washing the windows outside my 28th-story office and think, *I'd rather do that*—even though I am terrified of heights.

Now, I know many people who don't believe they are in the right career. Because where they are is not the pinnacle of their aspirations, they decide to do nothing productive in that space. They apply themselves minimally, just enough so they don't get fired. Or, they work a little bit more than the minimum, but they resent everyone around them for it (and maybe even themselves). I could have gone that direction. I certainly knew I was not where I belonged or where I wanted to be, even if I couldn't yet articulate where it was I thought I *did* belong. The position wasn't inspiring or impressive, and it definitely didn't provide me with a gigantic paycheck.

Instead, I utilized my bias for action: Even though I found my job torturous, I showed up every day, early and with a good attitude. I've learned that right there is a key to success that will put you ahead of nearly everyone else in the game. Looking back, I know that if I had not done my best, if I had chosen to sleep in, show up late, and drain my coworkers of any remaining enthusiasm they were clinging to, I would not have been cultivating character; I would have been cultivating failure. Instead, I kept looking for ways to take action, and pretty soon, the opportunities started knocking on my door.

A year into my time at Life of Georgia, the executives decided the company needed to cut costs and create efficiencies, so they hired a management consultant named John Drago to lead the initiative and selected a few employees to support it. To this day, I am not exactly sure who recommended me—maybe it was somebody who noticed I was bright and had good people skills; or, maybe it was the head of the Underwriting Department who thought it was a good way to get rid of me since I wasn't very good at my job and he likely knew I hated it—but lo and behold, that's what happened.

And thank God it did, because it led to the best thing to ever happen to me. As I was transferring out of the world of underwriting, my replacement was hired. That person turned out to be my future wife, Loveanne. She started at the company in early 1981 and we started dating not long after that; by May of 1982, we were married. (Talk about a bias for action!)

Professionally, I was also now on a track for success. Under John Drago's instruction and guidance, my new job was to study various departments and make presentations to senior management with our findings and recommendations. Not only did this give me valuable experience and exposure to the company's leadership, it turned out that I was very good at the work. I started to think maybe becoming a professional consultant like John would be a good direction to pursue. He was in his mid-50s and clearly was making good money. At lunch one day, I asked him what I needed to do to get started. He told me to get my MBA. That led me to enroll at Georgia State University.

When I was about to start taking night classes and shortly before my wedding, I moved into the condo Loveanne and I had decided to rent. It didn't take me long to realize that I was spending a whole lot of time commuting back and forth from home to work and home to school; so, I decided to look for a new job in a more convenient location. I saw an advertisement in the paper looking for young business analysts to man the new home office of A.L. Williams & Associates, another insurance company. I interviewed, they offered me a job with a better salary, and the rest is history.

Well, not quite.

After I turned in my resignation letter, the Executive Vice President called me into his office. By that point, he had become a bit of a personal hero of mine at Life of Georgia. He proceeded to tell me all the reasons why I should stay: Life of Georgia was an established company, while A.L. Williams was a fly-by-night outfit; here, I was well-known and well-liked; blah, blah, blah. The one thing he *didn't* do was offer me more money.

I didn't know if what he said about A.L. Williams was true or not and, frankly, I didn't care all that much. The new job was closer to home and was going to pay me $3,000 more than I was currently making. I only had to make it work for three years and then I'd be done with my MBA and could move on anyway.

As it turned out, A.L. Williams and its company culture turned out to be a great fit for my skill set and personal nature. I started there in 1982. In 2000, I became co-CEO. By that point, Life of Georgia was no more. It had been sold to another company and its operations closed.

By the time I answered that ad in the paper and showed up

on A.L. William's doorstep, I had spent one year showing up early, with a positive, can-do attitude, and a willingness to do whatever it took to get to where I wanted to go; and another year honing and demonstrating skills that would help me do anything I wanted to. Action begets action. If you want positive changes to happen in your life, you need to be positive and hone your inclination to act. You have to be willing to keep moving forward with a positive attitude, even when your present circumstances are less than ideal. If you doubt me, consider this:

Because of my time with Life of Georgia, I met Loveanne, with whom I have had an amazing life and created an incredible family, including two sons and four grandchildren. I finished my masters in business administration degree. And, after thirty-five years and a successful career at A.L. Williams, I finally reached that goal of becoming a consultant (in my "retirement").

TAKE EVERY OPPORTUNITY

"Inspiration is for amateurs. The rest of us just show up and get to work. If you wait around for the clouds to part and a bolt of lightning to strike you in the brain, you are not going to make an awful lot of work. All the best ideas come out of the process; they come out of the work itself."
~Chuck Close (painter & artist)

Sometimes, finding the motivation to succeed can be a challenge, especially if you feel unappreciated, overlooked, or underpaid. What we often don't realize is that we can build our motivation by choosing our own metric for success. Let's say you work in a restaurant and it's that time of night to roll napkins and silverware. You may see this as an inconvenience or maybe the bane of your very existence, but if you look at each roll as a singular success, you have a whole lot of opportunity in front of you. With attention to detail, care, and a little focus, you can cultivate success over and over. No one may notice, and likely no one will tell you that you did an amazing job, but you will know you succeeded at a task that required some small degree of fortitude to stick it out.

I learned that when I made an effort to be productive, even when I was tired, even when I was wholly uninspired, and even when I was overworked, I was rewarded with more responsibility and, oftentimes, *better* responsibility. If you think about it, the rate at which people give you responsibility in your life is a metric for your ability to succeed. If people see you can't succeed, even with the smallest of tasks, they certainly aren't going to give you something bigger and better to try your hand at.

What differentiated me from some of my coworkers (although not from all, because the good Lord knows I had leaders all around me showing me the way) was that I seized every opportunity. I said yes to everything. Every optional meeting, I chose to attend. Every training that I could get under my belt, I was there. I asked every question I could ask, even some I thought I already knew the answer to. I learned as much as I could about the processes, the people, and the business that was in front of me. I didn't wait for inspiration; I got to work.

I won't lie; in the beginning, some of my days at A.L. Williams were less than spellbinding. It was another insurance company. Every day was not filled with riveting exchanges and awe-inspiring enthusiasm for the company's mission. But, more days were filled with those things than not *because I chose to see it that way.* I chose to take a life course in the insurance business, *our* insurance business, and to develop a fascination for learning anything and everything. In that way, my days *were* riveting. My mind was engaged. As I learned about the company and its goals, I got to help the higher-ups more regularly, and that was exciting.

I was not in Art Williams's inner circle at his company. I always had someone higher than me to whom I answered, but I did support Art directly many times. What's more, I observed the goings on around the company, and I always asked *why*. No matter what move Art told us to make, I was asking myself, *Now why did he do that? What is he trying to achieve with that tactic?* Or, *What benefit will come to the rest of us because of that change he implemented?* So even when I was not in a position to call the shots, I was looking at why the person who called the shots was doing what they were doing. If I could understand how they acted and, more importantly, why they chose certain actions, I could hone my ability to take informed action in the future.

My bias for action enabled me to grab hold of every opportunity that came my way, even if the opportunity was thinking about why things were the way they were. As a result, I demonstrated to the higher-ups that I was eager to learn, invested in my work, and invested in the company itself. Regardless of where you come from, a good employer will always appreciate the ability to learn, adapt, and develop. Even if you don't fit in with a company's culture completely, if you exhibit a willingness to learn with enthusiasm and you support others on their learning journey, you will stand out, even if certain tasks prove to be challenging for you.

POLISHING YOUR SKILL SET

At some point in time, most of us find ourselves in jobs that don't showcase our best skills. Sometimes the bills just need to get paid. However, even in those positions, there is great importance in showing up and developing character so those opportunities don't go to waste. Realize that not every job that's a waste of your talent is a waste of your time. Read that again, just in case you missed it. You can cultivate growth within yourself whether you're being put to excellent use as an employee or not.

Knowing what your skill set is will help you in this world immensely. Maybe you think your skills aren't traditional or you aren't even sure what skills you have. Well, it's time to do some self-reflection and figure it out. Because, trust me, you do have skills, even if they are untapped. There are plenty of good workbooks out there to help you discern them. Your parents may also be a good source for insight into your skills. They might remember when you were in third grade and they first realized you had a knack for storytelling. That spelling bee you won when you were five? They remember. What skills did it take for you to achieve those early successes? I bet you still have them.

You have to be able to figure out your skill set, either on your own or with the help of someone who knows you well. If you do ask for someone else's opinion, you also have to know when to agree or disagree. I have a good friend who always told me I was organized. I am many things, but organized, I am not. So I listened to his great compliment and assessment of me (and thanked him), but I knew then like I know now that organizational skills are not my strong suit.

Knowing what you do well allows you to go out into the world and start doing well while you serve others. There are many online resources, including my Leadership Superpower Quiz—among hundreds of thousands of others—that can help you figure out where you might shine in the world of employment.

The trick is realizing that your "dream job" isn't really the goal. After all, you may not land that dream job right away, or maybe even at all … ever. (I'll wait a moment while you contemplate that.) Sometimes, getting what you think you want isn't the right thing for you. The real key to success is uncovering your best skills and your strongest assets and putting them to work in a place where you can grow, help others, and have some opportunities for advancement or networking based on those skills. Once you can find fulfillment in daily interactions as you become service-oriented, then the dream job isn't as important as it used to be because you are growing where you're planted.

One other note about so-called "dream jobs": Even if it looks like easy money, I guarantee you it's going to take work. In life, the only thing you get for nothing is nothing, so if you have a dream job in mind, you need a plan to get there and the skill set to get the job done.

Today, so many young people want to be social media influencers for a living, or they want to be YouTube stars. While I personally have no desire to ever be "influenced" by anyone on social media, I can objectively say that these people work their butts off. Their careers require a specialized skill set: They need creativity to build and expand their online personas and a talent for branding and design. They need to be tech-savvy to keep their accounts up-to-date and functioning. They need a basic understanding of photography and videography, along with editing and editing software. They have to be able to write, spell, and edit copy for video descriptions. They have to be able to storyboard their videos or create graphics to accompany posts. And that's just the start of it.

If you don't know how to do any of these things, you likely aren't going to make it to the level of success at which you can pay someone else to do it for you. Take another look at all those skills that are listed above. A person who can do all of that is a competent person. I would say that if most kids knew how much work actually goes into their favorite YouTuber's channel, they might not want to be an influencer at all. It is a lot of work. *Success* is a lot of work!

Another thing to consider for any of you burgeoning influencers out there: You can put your skills to work and develop a huge online presence, and that is one level of achievement; but there is another level you can strive for. Are you using your influence for good? Helping people and being of service is next-level success. Don't stop growing your skills once you hit a certain number of proverbial likes. You can use your talents to drive change in the world, and *that* is an influencer who is also practicing real leadership.

When developing any new skill or pursuing a new career, I recommend you start with what you know. You'll find so much success in life comes from simply knowing what you do well, where you shine, and then doing that. To be clear, I am not saying you shouldn't try new things or learn new skills; we need to do these things anyway to grow and to keep our minds sharp. But if we start down a new path armed with a recognition of our existing strengths and skills and how those assets can help us in our pursuits, then we are already armed for success.

Sometimes being realistic about our strengths can be tricky. There may be times when you sell yourself short and need to give yourself more credit. I find this to be especially true of folks for whom fear and uncertainty are familiar companions. If you're feeling doubtful about your skills and abilities, ask yourself the following: Have I done everything I reasonably can to be as good as I need to be to get the job done well? If the answer is yes, give yourself a break; you're doing fine.

You also have to be willing to admit when the skills you want to have (or maybe even those you think you have) are not quite up to par. I'm imagining the folks who go on the talent shows to sing, only to have the audience cringe as soon as they open their mouth. Sure, they have enthusiasm. Sure, they have desire. Sure, they have some talent, like courage, maybe showmanship, and passion for what they want to do. At some point, though, they have to admit to themselves that they need to pursue another avenue for their talents. Life is hard. What can I say?

Let's leave those people to their own devices while we dissect what it looks like to uncover heaps of individual skills.

Take a young man who plays guitar and wants to make a living playing music. He may argue that the only thing he is good at is playing the guitar and say, "I'm either going to be a star and get discovered, or I'm not." But he also knows how to organize and set up sound equipment, which is not a skill we all have. He knows how to play, which is something that he might use to make some money as he teaches others how to play, too. He knows how to write songs and how to make lyrics fit together nicely, so perhaps he could help others who struggle with the creative process of songwriting along the way.

If he wants to make money doing things he is good at, I see lots of opportunities for him to shine as he works toward his goals. Whether he meets the Eagles in a restaurant late one night and they recruit him as their new guitarist is up to fate; but today, he can put his skills to good use and make a living with those additional skills. It might not look exactly like his dream coming true, but it is a step forward in a direction he is willing to work for, and that makes all the difference in the world.

JUST DO IT

When you get right down to it, it's pretty simple: Our fears and uncertainties can keep us from moving forward, but only if we let them. We have a choice in the matter. We can choose to believe in ourselves, and we can choose to step into the unknown. Once you make the choice, the only thing left to do is to *do it*.

Long before Nike adopted "Just Do It" as their slogan, my mentor and hero, Art Williams, was giving a speech with that same exact name and sentiment. (Don't believe me? Look it up. You'll find it in multiple places on YouTube and across the Internet. The A.L. Williams attorneys were sure to notify Nike to let them know in no uncertain terms that Art would *not* be relinquishing the right to use the phrase.) Art's main point, which I wholeheartedly agree with, was that many people love to talk about what they're going to do, but very few actually do it. If you want results, if you want to win, *you have to do the work*. There will always be excuses and reasons to wait or not try. But even if the weather's bad, or your dog ate one of your best dress shoes, or you don't know where to start, or even if—Heaven forbid—you get lost because you read the map incorrectly, if you have a goal that you want to achieve, you had best get after it. You have to fight to win.

One of my favorite Art quotes is, "Winners win and losers lose." It may sound harsh, but the older I get, the more wholly and completely I believe it to be true. You could give certain people ten million dollars and they would find a way to lose it. But if you act, and start moving in the direction of your goal; if you persist and don't quit—when you win that prize? You will be primed and ready to fight to keep it.

When you develop a bias for action, when you decide to be the rolling stone that gathers no moss, the universe will assist you. It will harmonize with your purpose and your goals as long as you make an effort and find some gratitude along the way.

I have found that most of the struggles in life can be solved with a correction of perception. When it feels like you aren't getting the opportunities you want, consider that you're getting the opportunities *you need* in order to grow to get to where you want to be. If you struggle with patience, you're probably going to attract a lot of barking dogs, noisy children, and customer service representatives who keep putting you on hold until you turn old and gray. Why? Because those are the things that build patience. You can't develop a skill or turn a shortcoming into a strength without the opportunity to do so. That is where you have to shift your mental habit from frustration to appreciation.

Each challenge is what you make of it. If you sit around in fear that you will never overcome the obstacles in your life, I guarantee that you will never overcome the obstacles in your life. But if you see them as small, individual opportunities to succeed and to grow, and you start taking action in the direction of helping others as well as yourself, you will discover that fear doesn't fit as comfortably in your life. After all, fear is just the tenant who keeps that dark room in the basement, and you, my friend, are now in the process of renovating your whole house.

9

FLIPPING THE SCRIPT ON FEAR

Many of my fondest memories as a child are of playing in the forest around our home. With not many other children around, I would turn to my imagination to keep me busy. Aside from reading books and watching movies, those hours in the woods playing Robin Hood and James Bond were how I spent most of my time. It was simple. It was magical.

Back in 1967, when I was ten years old, Six Flags Over Georgia burst onto the scene in Atlanta. Those were the days when driving into the bustling city didn't come with an unavoidable extra hour or two of traffic, so my parents and our family friends made the trip to the amusement park a regular outing. Every visit, like clockwork, the adults insisted on heading to the same spot in the park for some good old-fashioned Southern grub: fried chicken, mashed potatoes, green beans—the whole shebang. Now, I grew up on Southern cuisine. Cornbread was a staple on our dinner table. And don't get me wrong, it sounds downright delicious now; but back then, I was bored with the norm. To my young eyes, Six Flags was supposed to be all about thrilling new experiences. I craved adventure, and I was determined to find it.

While exploring the Spanish-themed section of the park, I discovered a little Mexican restaurant. I had zero exposure to Mexican food at that point in my life, and that was exactly the kind of adventure I was yearning for. I mustered up all my persuasive skills to convince my parents to part with some cash, and then I made my way to that cozy cantina to order the most exotic thing I could conceive of: empanadas and chips. As I waited for my order, I looked around and imagined myself in a foreign place, far from Six Flags Over Georgia of Atlanta, where I was seeing the world through new eyes and experiencing it through new senses. Standing in the courtyard of that replica Spanish fort, the Castillo de Soto, I had discovered a whole new world within my world and gained a new perspective on everything around me.

While locating and procuring exotic cuisine was one part of the familiar trip I had to find a solution for, there was another prominent thing impacting my ability to have fun at Six Flags: my debilitating fear of heights. I knew I was finally tall enough to ride the Dahlonega Mine Train roller coaster, but I had a hard time even walking past the stubby sign reading "You Must Be This Tall to Ride." In my mind, everyone waiting in the queue was lined up to jump off the edge of a cliff. You know the age-old question, "If all your friends jumped off a cliff, would you?" The answer for me has always been a resounding "No!", for more reasons than one. It's evolution, after all, not to want to die. Yet, despite thinking those people might be a few cards short of a full deck, I *was* envious of them. After all, riding roller coasters is a rite of passage for young lads such as myself.

I began contemplating a way to conquer the towering rides that loomed over the park. They were intimidating, but I yearned for the thrill and the camaraderie of sharing in the fun with my friends. The more I thought about it, I found myself questioning my perspective on fear itself.

What if, instead of avoiding fear or seeing it as something to be conquered, I welcomed it as valuable information—neutral data, neither good nor bad? What if I could convince myself that fear didn't need to alter who I was, limit my aspirations, or impede my journey toward them? What if there was a way to stop fear from taking over and gripping my mind like a viper with a mouse? What if I could think my way free of fear?

I wasn't sure what the answer was or if it was possible, but I was certainly going to investigate.

Now, you may be expecting this story to end with me hopping on the tallest ride in the park and quashing my fear once and for all, but that isn't what happened. In fact, it took me several more decades before I could bring myself to ride a roller coaster (now, I love them!). But that day, in contemplating doing something I was terrified of, I realized the important thing was not whether I conquered my fear through confrontation; rather, *it was the ability to understand and reshape my relationship with that fear.* Riding the roller coaster would have been a symbolic act (a cool one, at that), but it wouldn't have fundamentally altered my relationship with fear or provided me with any profound insights. I was searching for lasting change to this problem of fear, and in fact, I had found exactly what I was looking for.

By choosing not to challenge my fear head-on that day, I discovered a different kind of bravery: the courage to accept myself, fear and all, to make choices that genuinely resonated with my innermost values and desires.

BOVINE BRAVERY

I hear you saying, "John, that's all well and good. But what happens when the thing you fear doing absolutely must be done anyway?" In these cases, the best advice I can give is, sometimes you just need to lean into the fear and let it propel you *into* action. That may sound crazy and counterintuitive, but even nature offers us examples of why this tactic works.

When I was growing up, I once heard that the difference between how cattle and bison approach storms determines how many in each herd will survive. Intrigued, I decided to learn more.

It turns out that, when dark clouds gather and thunder rolls across the vast plains, striking fear into the hearts of all the grassland creatures, cattle will usually get spooked and run from the storm. They run with the wind, ahead of the weather front. Instinctively, this makes sense, to run from the storm and from the perceived danger. And yet, if they run and scatter, they actually incur *more* injury and death because they are exposed to the elements for a longer period of time. There is a greater likelihood of them getting separated (especially calves from their mothers), which makes them easy targets for predators. And, even if they don't run or scatter, they tend to gather into a large herd, hoping that safety in numbers will protect them; unfortunately, in a big herd, they attract lightning, and that's not good.

Bison, however, have a different instinctive approach to storms, one that can teach us a lot about turning our fears into fuel. Unlike cattle, when a storm approaches, a herd of bison will walk (if not run) straight into it. Bison have an innate understanding that going *into* the storm will get them through it faster than running from it. They pass quickly through the edge of the storm so as to limit exposure to the most violent winds, which can whip up dangerous projectiles that could possibly harm their eyes, one of the most vulnerable organs on which they rely for survival. Now, nothing against cows here, but for a member of the bovine species, that's pretty smart.

One of Winston Churchill's most famous quotes is, "If you are going through Hell, keep going." Maybe Churchill knew what the bison knew; I honestly couldn't tell you. What I do know is this: If we can shift our perspective around fear and change our approach to it, then we can see life's approaching storms not as reasons to run or hide, but as opportunities to face head-on, plow through, and minimize our time in the thunder and lightning.

I don't know about you, but anything that makes life's storms shorter sounds pretty appealing to me.

SEEING FEAR FOR WHAT IT IS

Physiologically speaking, fear is the impulse to do or not do something in the interest of survival. It is our biological warning system, saying, "CAUTION: this might hurt." To this very day, I can still hear Momma's words: "Don't touch that stove, Johnny!" She was afraid I might not be scared enough of something that could hurt me, so she shared her fear until I could develop my own, and I did.

People who are older and wiser have shared their fears with us throughout our lives, and whether we know it or not, their relationship with fear has influenced us. Sometimes, as in the hot stove scenario above, it is clear when someone shares a fear with us, and sometimes it's not as obvious.

My nanny, Edith Addison, was the most wonderful grandmother a boy could hope for. (We called her "Nanny" because she didn't want to be "Granny.") She was funny and smart as a whip. I loved her dearly, and we went on lots of adventures together. I cherished our time together, and I watched her closely —*very* closely, in fact. On top of being an amazing human being and the world's best nanny, she also had an irrational fear of germs.

By itself, her germophobia didn't seem like that big of a deal to me. Sure, she washed her hands so many times a day that they were always red, but that was about it as far as I could tell. Then, in the 1960s, something changed. Almost overnight, Nanny became absolutely crippled by the fear of cancer. More specifically, she developed an irrational fear of cancer being contagious. No scientific study, doctor's word, or anything else could convince her otherwise. She and my granddaddy were just simple country people; the idea of going to a therapist was a non-starter. She was certain that cancer was contagious and everyone else was needlessly and dangerously exposing themselves, and that was that.

Nanny's fear was so bad that, when the husband of one of her dear, lifelong friends was diagnosed with cancer, she refused to visit them for fear of contracting cancer. She missed spending precious last weeks and days with some of her best friends because this fear had taken over her mind.

Maybe someone shared that erroneous, irrational fear with Nanny; we aren't sure. It's possible she heard cancer was contagious from someone at the beauty shop, grocery store, or a friend somewhere along the line. Maybe something she was told as a child made her feel that way, the comment laying dormant in her subconscious until it reared its ugly head many decades later. But no rational, reasonable, logical conversation could alleviate her concern and quell this fear in her heart that she would catch this most devastating of afflictions.

Fast forward to the early 1990s. Nanny and Granddaddy, well into their eighties by this point, were still living at home. My dad or his brother, my uncle Fred, would make weekly visits to check on them and make sure they had everything they needed. One week, around Christmastime, my father wasn't available to make the trip so I offered to go. When I arrived, I found my granddaddy all in a dither, trying to make a phone call to 911. Nanny had fallen in the kitchen and broken a hip.

After I took the phone from Granddady and gave the emergency operator the address, I set about trying to keep my grandparents calm as we waited for an ambulance. I recall sitting with Nanny, trying to offer her comfort, but she was panicked. If I tried to place a hand on her shoulder or to make her more comfortable, she would yell, "Don't touch me, I'm dirty!" That just about broke my heart.

Before too long, the paramedics arrived to take Nanny to the hospital. Not wanting to leave Granddaddy alone at the house, I stayed with him for about an hour until my uncle could get there. By the time I arrived at the hospital, Nanny was already settled in a room. As I walked down the hallway, I steeled myself for whatever it was I might be walking into. This was Nanny—my germaphobic, cancer-fearing nanny—*in a hospital*. I knew it wasn't going to be pretty.

Well. I'm glad I didn't bet the farm on that one, because I would have lost, big time.

When I walked through the door, there was Nanny, sitting up in bed and chatting away with a nurse, just as calm as could be. There were no hysterics. There was no talk of germs or catching cancer. It was just my kind, loving nanny showing appreciation for the staff that were helping her. It was the most amazing thing. Must've been the pain medication, right? Wrong.

Nanny was relaxed for the duration of her hospital stay. Then, when she was moved to the nursing facility next door, again I thought, *here we go*. I figured she'd go downhill quickly at a place like that. But that's not what happened. Her fears were just … gone. No one had any explanation for it. After a short time, my granddaddy ended up at the nursing home with Nanny. They were able to spend their remaining days together without the heavy weight of Nanny's irrational (but very real) fears looming over them. It was nothing short of miraculous.

To this day, I don't know if it was a mini-stroke, some other medical anomaly, or honest-to-goodness divine intervention that "cured" Nanny of her fears of germs and cancer. I *do* know that, for most people with debilitating phobias, it doesn't seem to work this way.

I sincerely hope that whatever fears you are facing aren't so extreme. But regardless of severity, it's important to understand that this is how fear works: If left unchecked, it creates an invisible box around people. The walls grow closer and closer together as each day passes. Fear shrinks their world, limiting their ability to live their lives. It kills possibility, opportunity, and potential, which is actually very sad. When I think of the people whose time was cut short with Nanny because of her fear, I think of precious moments lost. Those lost moments made *me* want to get real about combatting the effects of fear in people's lives.

So, how do you know when fear is the useful kind that keeps you from stepping on snakes lying in wait in the grass or the useless kind that stops people from achieving their potential?

When determining if a fear is reasonable to entertain, it can be helpful to take an inventory. There are three general questions I ask myself that help me get a better perspective on fear: First, is this a fear that was given to me by someone else, or is it my own? Second, is it a rational or irrational fear? Third, will I let it dictate how I approach something or stop me from doing something altogether?

Put even more simply, is the fear mine? Is it real? Does it change anything?

Now, don't get me wrong: When you are in the fear-gripped throes of a crisis, asking any questions on a rational level won't likely be possible. So don't beat yourself up if you can't take this level-headed approach when you've got a spider crawling up your pant leg. This work of changing your perspective is meant for when you have time to think and when you can take a short dive into your psyche.

I was once invited to a very cool party by my good friend Stuart Johnson who used to own *SUCCESS* magazine. The event took place at the rooftop bar of a new hotel that was creating a lot of buzz in Dallas. I arrived just as the party was getting going. It was crowded, and I saw familiar faces everywhere I looked. After making my way to the bar and ordering my beverage of choice, I headed toward the balcony to speak with some friends and colleagues who were out there enjoying the view. I stepped outside to say hello … and just about had a heart attack.

It just so happens that the floor of this particular balcony was glass and, as you'll recall from the start of this chapter, I am not a fan of heights. Looking down to the ground some thirty stories below my feet just about did me in. Now, here I was, in front of all my friends (arguably some of the most successful people in the business world), sick with terror. All I could do, short of turning tail and running back inside, was press my back against the wall and try like heck to remain composed for the next ten minutes until I could return to the safety of tile flooring. I was embarrassed. It wasn't rational. I knew I was safe, yet I still panicked.

Don't be too hard on yourself if your newfound insights don't cause your fears to dissipate. Even if you understand a fear intimately, know exactly where it comes from, and can determine with certainty whether or not it's legitimate, there is no guarantee the fear is going to leave. Rather, the goal of the ideas I've shared is to flip the script, to *change our relationship to fear*.

Changing our relationship to fear is what gets us to the place where we can effect any change whatsoever. Before, we were simply unaware, reacting to things. Now, we can let awareness help us begin to change our minds about our fear as we contemplate the reality *and* validity of it.

A PLAN OF ACTION

American psychologist Susan Jeffers wrote a famous book called *Feel the Fear … and Do It Anyway*. That title expresses a powerful sentiment that is short, sweet, and to the point. Earlier we talked about the importance of having a bias for action. While your brain might tell you that fear should have some final say about what you choose to do or not do, I am a big fan of walking through fear and doing it anyway, whatever "it" is. Now, I'm not suggesting you climb down into a pit full of vipers purely for the sake of overcoming your fear of snakes. Unless someone has fallen into that pit and you are their only hope of rescue, it probably won't be necessary for you to do something so terrifying and dangerous. But there are some common, everyday fears that we must overcome in order to function in society.

Like most kids, I was petrified of shots. So when vaccines for deadly childhood diseases like polio, mumps, and measles came on the scene, I was in a pickle. I understood that, like it or not, I needed to get those shots. It wasn't an option to let my fear stop me from getting them—mainly because, unlike the decision of whether or not to ride a roller coaster, this choice wasn't one I had much say over; if the doctor *and* my mom said I needed shots, well, that was that. Eventually, I got over my fear of needles. The benefit of facing that particular fear when I was young is that I trained myself to do things that were good for me, even if I didn't enjoy them or was afraid of them.

That training came in handy when Rick Williams, my fellow co-CEO, and I were working on separating Primerica from Citigroup when the financial crisis happened in Fall 2008.

At that point, we had been working hard behind the scenes for nearly two years, looking for ways to get out from under the Citigroup umbrella. Citigroup, like all of the major financial firms in the 2000s, had become subject to increasingly onerous regulatory policies that were being applied to all of its divisions, including Primerica. The problem was, Primerica was not a bank, it was not structured like a bank, and it did not function like a bank. Being asked to comply with one new regulation after another that had no relevance to our business was slowly strangling the life out of us. Rick and I knew that Primerica would not survive, much less thrive, under this regime. Fortunately, Citi's leadership was willing to let Primerica go, provided it was under terms everyone could live with.

We were on the threshold of just such a deal when the financial collapse happened. In a matter of three days, everything

Rick and I and our leadership team had worked so incredibly hard for, went up in smoke. Now, not only was Primerica still tethered to Citigroup's sinking ship, but our people, especially those in the field, were looking at personal financial catastrophe. If we were going to survive as a company, we *had* to find a way out from under Citi.

It was at this point that the mantra, "When a door closes, go through a window" was playing on a loop in my head. With other people's livelihoods on the line, it was imperative that we find a way to forge ahead. The problem was, I had no idea where that darn window was and I was scared I wouldn't be able to find it. I would wake up at two in the morning, covered in sweat, in a dead panic. The tremendous doubt in my head would ask, "Who do you think you are to lead this company during one of the biggest financial crises in recent history?" Then, I would think, *God, am I good enough to do this? Am I good enough at what I do to make this happen?* I was living in a war zone that was centered a few inches above my neck, right between my ears. And if the war is that close to home, you know there's no walking away from it.

You might have heard of "analysis paralysis." This can happen when we face high stakes and have multiple or murky options in front of us, none of which is an obvious "best" option. We become paralyzed with indecision out of fear of making the wrong choice. Analyzing our fears can be a helpful tool; it can provide us with transformative insight. But sometimes, it's just another way to let fear live rent-free in our heads and hinder our ability to move forward.

So here I was, wracked with self-doubt and fear. I knew I had to overcome my fear of not being good enough, smart enough, or capable enough to get Primerica out of Citigroup, because people were counting on me. As long as I live, I will never forget what it was like to have the weight of that responsibility on my shoulders.

You see, Primerica is one company made up of many, many

other businesses—other businesses with their own teams and their own sales forces, made up of thousands of people with countless family members and loved ones who rely on those businesses for their livelihoods. This situation wasn't just a matter of what was best for me or Rick or the company we ran; it was about what was best for *all* of them. Letting analysis paralysis take hold was not an option. I needed to do as Susan Jeffers said: Feel the fear and do it anyway.

It's important to understand that Rick and I both could have taken a check to bide our time, just to keep things together for a few more years while Citigroup figured out what to do with Primerica. In all likelihood, it would have meant the end of our company. Even so, no one would have blamed us if we chose to just go along and let Citi call the shots. With the market in shambles and the company going through the worst period in its entire history, the deck was stacked against us. The easier path, failure, was ours for the taking. But we knew what it would mean to our friends and our Primerica family if we chose the deal Citi was offering us, and that was just plain unacceptable. Rick and I were different in many ways—he was the yin to my yang; the calm, reflective one who could balance my more reactive, passionate tendencies—but on this point we were in complete agreement

I recall one particularly difficult conversation during this time with the Citigroup executive in charge of managing the deal. He was trying to convince us of the financial sense in what they were offering. He had charts and graphs and the whole nine yards. But I had had enough. "Look," I said. "I get what you're saying. But you are talking about numbers on a spreadsheet. I am fighting for families' *lives*. My motivation here is stronger than yours. That's just a fact."

There's more to this story, but for now the important thing to realize is that I knew if I had given in to my fear, Primerica never would have left Citigroup. Had that happened, hundreds of thousands of people would have been negatively impacted by my inability to walk forward despite my knocking knees. I knew that the doubters, the ones living both inside and outside of my head, were the ones I was sent to prove wrong. I had to convince myself to keep plugging away, no matter what. I have seen the reward on the other side of fear, and I know we are capable of so much more than we think we are, even when we are scared to death.

You *can* find a way to make yourself do something. When the stakes are high and something absolutely must be done (whether it's getting your shots or standing up to a global giant that has the power to crush all you've built), you must find a way to push forward. As hockey legend Wayne Gretzky said, "You miss one hundred percent of the shots you don't take."

While fear is that natural impulse to do or not do something, you have the power to make choices in spite of it. The more you get into the habit of making your choices despite fear, the more capable you become at not letting it rule you or your life. The more you walk through your fears and act anyway, the more you see that fear doesn't have to be a factor at all when it comes to decision-making. At that point, you have turned your fear into fuel by realizing your power over it.

HISTORY PROPELS US FORWARD

While Franklin Delano Roosevelt's quote "The only thing we have to fear is fear itself" was popularized during his 1933 inauguration speech as he hoped to bring America through the Great Depression, those words were not exclusively his. The idea and the words have been expressed by historical giants who were Roosevelt's predecessors, such as Francis Bacon, Henry David Thoreau, and, foremost, French writer Michel de Montaigne. Many exceptional people throughout millennia have seen their way around or through fear and done amazing things. However, you don't need to be a great thinker or writer to make those words your motto; you only need to be committed to seeing the truth of things, which will be enough.

As a young student, I got good grades and did well in school overall. I had wonderful friends and maintained good relationships. I liked my teachers and they liked me. School was a positive thing in my life, so there was no good reason why I didn't want to go to college. The truth was, I didn't want to leave my life, my friends, and my girlfriend. Life was good in Covington; I was comfortable there. At seventeen years old, I couldn't see a decent reason why I needed to leave that comfort zone, but it seemed like it was going to happen anyway. When it was time, I took my SATs and did well enough to be accepted to the University of Georgia, where, in theory at least, I had always dreamed of going, and so that appeared to be the next logical step for me.

You might recall from chapter two how things turned out. What I experienced when I got to UGA was the opposite of my prior school experience. I felt different from everyone else, like they belonged but I did not. I felt like everyone was smarter than me. I was certain that all of them had been prepared for their college experience in some way that I had not.

On the first day of my Political Science 101 class, a girl seated in the row in front of me asked whether or not we would be getting a syllabus. A syllabus? I had never heard that word and had no clue what it meant. I was terrified and disappointed in myself.

Self-doubt was running me over like a freight train every darn day.

In my first few weeks at UGA, life gave me a thousand reasons to fail. I could have walked away on my first day of classes, come home, and gotten a job. I would have been back with my friends and my girlfriend ... and my life would have turned out altogether different than it did. I'm pretty happy now and, looking back, I see that syllabus situation as a decision point in my life. It was a critical instant in which I was about to make or break my entire future. I could have chosen failure.

Instead, I finished that first semester and transferred to the smaller Oxford College of Emory University to get my feet back under me. I returned to UGA my junior year with renewed confidence and completed my degree as a proud Georgia Bulldog.

That's life for you. It will always give you ample reasons to quit and ample opportunities to fail. You, yourself, have to be the reason that you don't. No one else can carry you. It's entirely up to you.

On the morning of June 6, 1944, General Dwight D. Eisenhower, Supreme Allied Commander, was holding his breath. Despite the worst forecast he could have imagined around the beaches of Normandy, France, a small window appeared in which the weather would be decent enough to send troops ashore. After visiting with the troops the day prior, he had been given a piece of paper with the statistic that this invasion carried with it an 80% rate of casualty. Well over half of the men he had just met and chatted with about their families and hobbies would never come home; but he knew the consequences of inaction would be much worse. Nazi Germany had taken hold, and, at times, it appeared as though a win for the Allied troops was nowhere near certain.

I don't envy anyone who has to make choices that determine whether people live or die, and in Eisenhower's case, it wasn't a matter of *if* but *how many* people would die. He could either invade and lose an astounding number of men in the process, or he could wait for more countries to be invaded, which he knew would lead to countless more lives lost. Can you imagine how frightening that must have been?

Before the troops landed on the beaches that morning, Eisenhower wrote a letter to the American public that, fortunately, never had to be shared. The last words of that letter read, "If any blame or fault attaches to the attempt, it is mine alone."

While I have never carried the weight of potential casualties as a consequence of my choices, in deciding whether or not to quit college and whether or not to quit fighting for Primerica, the blame for those failures would have rested with me alone. On D-Day, Eisenhower faced a high likelihood of failure, but he chose to forge ahead, and success reigned.

If you want to succeed, you can't let your past or present govern your future. You can let them inform, enhance, empower, and even inspire your decisions, but allowing them to dictate your future will ensure that you stay inside the mental box you have put yourself in. That box is what you make of it. Your personal history can absolutely propel you forward, ever closer to what you want to achieve; or, you can let it confuse you about what you are capable of. Don't allow your fears, doubts, and uncertainties to limit the size of your dreams. You are greater than that, and we both know it.

HOW DO YOU LIKE ME NOW?

Kirby Smart, head coach of the Georgia Bulldogs (and one of my favorite people on the planet), likes to quote Henry David Thoreau to his champion team: "Success usually comes to those who are too busy to be looking for it." Boy, isn't that the truth? When you are busy making it happen, moving forward, and getting after it, success can't help but appear as a side effect. The problem is that many people stop to let fear deter them, slow them down, and make them hesitate to take that next step.

It is a fact that the moment you are experiencing right now is about to become the past. If you aren't one hundred percent in love with this moment, then you can make a new plan for the future. What do you want to change, and how can you change it? If you aren't changing it, you are choosing it. Don't just think about where you want to be ten years from now; think about that *and* make a plan you can begin implementing ten minutes from now that will get you to your destination.

When you choose to figure out how to succeed ten minutes from now, and another ten minutes from then, and so on, all those minutes sure do add up. Before you know it, you have stockpiled an awful lot of successes.

In my mind, incremental success is the only kind anyone should be worried about. I am not the same person I was back in college, nor am I the same person I was in my early days with A.L. Williams. That's because I spent a lot of time focusing on how I could be better than I was in the next moment, and the next, and then the next. I wasn't worried about the future in the grand scheme of things; I was worried about how I could just be a little bit better, day by day. I wasn't worried about how I could be perfect, either, because striving for perfection is another dangerous and paralyzing opponent in the fear game.

Just as the real success that matters is incremental, I believe the term "perfection" should only be used in relation to how things taste, how gardens flourish, and the Georgia Bulldogs' football team. If you are using the word "perfect" as your standard to measure yourself against, well, I'll tell you how that will work out: It won't. At least, it never has for me.

To put it another way, success is about progress, not perfection. How much progress you make in any one area depends on how much effort you put into it. Admittedly, it can be hard—if not impossible—to act when staring down fears and anxieties that overwhelm you. When you are afraid, especially when you are faced with paralyzing fear, thinking too much about the perfect outcome you want in the future is probably the worst thing you can do (second only to hurling yourself off a cliff). Fear narrows our vision, making big things seem impossible. If you choose to focus on the small, incremental successes that get you just one step further along your path than you were before, the thought of making big things happen becomes less overwhelming.

Every time we choose to act in spite of fear and engage in regular, incremental action that gets us closer to our goals, we are telling fear that we won't be stopped. We are saying, "See, fear? I recognize you. I know you are comfortable here and may not leave, but I am not going to quit, either. I am going to keep going, keep fighting, and you can try to convince me of anything you want to, but I am not quitting or changing course, no matter what you say." As long as you are still moving forward, even if it's from second to second and inch by inch, you are still fighting the good fight.

In my mind, progress *is* perfection. I'll bet you didn't see that coming, but think about it: That small shift in how you think about perfection might be the one change you need to make in order to get out of your own way and make all your dreams come true. Now, go get after it.

10

WHAT IS REQUIRED

REVEL IN FAILURE?

Right now, so much political change is happening that it's mind-blowing. Every time I turn on the TV, I am flabbergasted. Our world has been reshaped over and over in such a short period that it is rather unprecedented. I can think of dozens of folks I know who would really be serving the greater good by running for office. They are all capable of making necessary advances and instituting the kind of change and reform that would likely stabilize much of the instability pervading our government today.

When I ask why they don't run, they respond with things like, "John, who am I to make that kind of change?" With that attitude, they are nobody. But with the courage and ability to face their fears and take charge of their capacity to inspire and lead, they could be who everyone else needs them to be. If they took that kind of risk, they might fail. Sure, that's a real possibility.

But think about the world of opportunity that would open up if they chose to face that fear, run for office, and they won.

Their voices, their ideas, and their positive ambitions would finally be center stage. They could effect all sorts of change, really help people, and bring fresh perspectives to what's going on, as long as they don't think, *Who am I to do XYZ?* Who they are is THE person or persons, the ones we might all need to reshape the world.

When we make an effort to step in any new direction, there's a chance that we will fail or succeed. But when we choose not to act because of a fear of failure, we have already ensured the very thing we were trying to avoid in the first place.

Out of all the things I admire most about Winston Churchill, his ability to get back up and keep going after taking a backroad beating is at the top of that list. Remember back in chapter three, where I mentioned his big military debacle while trying to invade Gallipoli during the First World War? He was ousted from the British Admiralty after making a call that cost the lives of 46,000 Allied troops. After the failure, he picked up a weapon and headed to France's front lines. In his mind, his political career was over … until one day, it wasn't. Despite his tremendously humiliating political setback, change continued to call to him, and he couldn't tell his destiny to step aside because he was too afraid he might be embarrassed again politically. In fact, he was sure he would be embarrassed at some point, but that did not stop him.

When running for Parliament in 1923, hecklers threw the failure at the Dardanelles in Churchill's face. They taunted and teased him publicly, harassing him and saying terrible things about his tactics, his choices, and his overall fitness to lead. They were attempting to disrupt his equilibrium enough to get him to drop out of the race, but what they didn't count on was Winston being Winston. While he was not proud of the lives lost that day, he knew that the previous "failure" might have saved the lives of millions. He took a gamble and lost; that was it. He didn't punish or mentally flog himself for decades, never to return and face the public again. He knew he had taken a calculated risk, and his calculation had simply not panned out.

So, how did he flip the script on fear? Churchill told everyone that he embraced the brilliant failure of the Dardanelles rather than running from it. He knew there had been potential for success, even after a failure of that magnitude.

Imagine yourself in Churchill's shoes at that time. You've just been formally chastised and very publicly removed from your post as the First Lord of the Admiralty. You have run to another country and taken up arms. You are cold, muddy, and watching your friends and fellow soldiers die around you. It might seem hopeless. How could you have fallen so far?

However, you've been granted a gift in this; you know what the worst of the worst looks like. You have seen the face of war up close and personal. You now know exactly why you are fighting and what (and probably who) you are fighting for. Churchill's tremendous failure was also a tremendous setup for an even more tremendous comeback. *That* is what success looks like when we turn our fear into fuel.

I am sure you have watched a movie in your life, maybe one or two. The plot usually looks fairly similar from one to the next if you strip it down to bare bones. You have your hero, and you have your villain. Their storylines cross; there is some conflict, they battle, and the hero loses. He returns home and licks his wounds. Dejected, he fears his ability to ever do anything of consequence again (save for getting a dog and drinking some beers).

As time marches on, something or someone reignites his belief in himself that he can save the day. He trains, he struggles, and he overcomes his struggles (this is usually a montage paired with excellent rock music). One day, he decides to pick up his mantle once more. He seeks out the villain who is now running the world, they battle, and usually, our hero wins the day on the second go 'round. It's a fairly well-worn pattern in the film industry.

But consider this: If our hero battles the villain and wins on the first try, we only have half a movie, and sometimes we don't even have that much. The development of the plot is the hero's struggle. Why? Because we can all relate to struggle and defeat. That's what makes us invest emotionally in the story. How boring would the world be if we succeeded at everything on our first try? There would be no growth, no character development, no self-reflection involved, just winning. But how could there be winning without losing?

Do you see where I'm going here? It's like the salt in the brownies that makes the sugar taste sweeter. Without defeat, without failure, without the salt in our brownies, life is a heck of a lot less sweet. It's consequently a heck of a lot less interesting, too. That's how I like to think about failure. It's a necessary part of growth whether we like it or not.

In life, we have to go through the mess to get to the message. As humans, moreover, as leaders, we have to understand that we all have the potential to turn right back around and overcome after a loss, even a devastating and humiliating one, but only if we dare to face that fear and walk right through it.

IMPACT IS IMPACT

I mentioned earlier that as a kid I wanted to do great things in my life, but I wasn't sure how, when, or what that would look like. Despite my initial plan for A.L. Williams to be a small stepping stone, I felt the impulse to get started moving toward where I thought I wanted to be. I started small, making the moves I could in the right direction. Before I knew it, all those small moves had amounted to something quite big. I was proud of myself for following that inner guidance and not being too afraid of the fact that these small advancements might not be big enough to satisfy my childhood thirst for greatness.

The truth is that great things come in all sizes. Starting small is always a good idea if you want to make positive changes in your life. As you experience more success in the small things that don't overwhelm your entire life, you can work toward bigger and better things if you want to.

You might be afraid that you will never be an influential leader at the national level, but that does not have to stop you from acting in your corner of the world. You may choose to start with your local grocers, cashiers, service staff, or anyone else with whom you come into contact. You have to be the person you want to become with everyone around you, no matter their station, overall impact, or influence on your life. Then, you'll start to notice your fears of not being as big as you might want to be dissolving. As you begin to observe your impact, you might receive some gratitude from the people whose lives you are positively influencing. Fully comprehending our impact on others, even on a very small scale, tends to override fears of not achieving overwhelming greatness. Sometimes, repeated small wins are just what the doctor ordered to keep us soldiering on.

When it comes to making lasting changes and approaching fears related to growth, one of the best things you can do is to grow where you're planted. When you commit to being the best you can be and show up as your best self, doors will open for you that you may have never expected. Once those doors start to open as a result of focusing on being your best right where you are, you will see opportunities for growth and upward movement that may very well surpass your expectations. If you make the best of what you've got right in front of you and right within you, better things and more growth opportunities will come your way.

Sometimes, you will have to ignore that fear that says, "You'll never make the kind of big impact you want to make," and start with making a smaller impact in a big way. As you start to experience regular achievement, no matter the size, any fear of not being able to reach your goals will ultimately recede in the presence of success. You don't have to win the presidency right off the bat, but you can begin your campaign on the smallest scale. Do not be deterred by what might feel like and appear to you as a lack of making a sufficient impact. Impact is impact. Don't forget: Every drop in the ocean raises the level of the water.

Believe me, when it comes to good, you aren't going to run out of causes to get behind or chances to make an impact. Crazy and bad people are still going to do crazy and bad things; you can choose to offset their influence by being one of the sane and good people who continue to do sane and good things. And, you can start on as small a scale as you need to while you build that confidence in overcoming your fears.

When it comes to making a difference, it's the good people who have to commit and dedicate themselves to making those changes. No matter where you come from, what your background is, or how badly you think you might fail due to your heaps of perceived ineptitude, stick with it. If you let fear stop you from starting, you let fear win. You sit, you soak, you get sour, and you complain about your circumstances. And if enough people let fear win, nothing in the world will ever change. In that way, all the good in the world, all the growth, and all the meaningful change starts with you. You have to feel the fear and *do it anyway*.

WHAT IS REQUIRED

We've already covered a bit of the story around Primerica's extrication from Citigroup (you can read the whole account in *Real Leadership*), but there is another chapter from that saga that I want to share.

It was 2009 and things were not going well. Every day, Rick and I would get news of what was happening within the Citi boardrooms that could mean the imminent destruction of everything we had worked so hard to create. As a company, we were staring into the abyss and that abyss was staring right back into us, assuring us that failure was imminent, there was no way out, and that our efforts would yield no fruit. At times, many times actually, it seemed completely hopeless.

One such point came while Rick and I were in New York to talk with Citigroup leadership about a new contract they wanted us to sign. They were offering us a significant payout to stick around for a few more years and keep things calm while the ship slowly sank around us. The big hitch was the non-compete clause. If we agreed to that, any leverage we held would go out the window. As you can imagine, we weren't too keen on that idea. Truth be told, we weren't keen on any of this—as I said earlier, what we cared about was protecting the livelihoods of the Primerica family. Period, full stop.

Well, in the midst of that larger negotiation, Citi broke the news that we needed to cancel all of the incentive trips and conventions we had in place for our teams. Like other financial giants at the time, Citigroup had received an infusion of federal TARP funds that were intended to prop up and stabilize the banks during the financial crisis; and now, certain companies were being publicly criticized for continuing to offer employee incentives with "government money."

I was flabbergasted at this announcement for two reasons: Number one, Primerica didn't need TARP money. Financially, our business was fine. Number two, incentives and large events are built into the company's business model. Primerica works because it uses exciting, fun events as incentives to motivate its giant sales force. We had a company trip to Atlantis in the Bahamas coming up. People had already met the requirements for the incentives to be in effect. Now we were being told to cancel it?

I lost it. I said, "I'm out of here, guys. Y'all are telling us to just go out of business. You've just unplugged the refrigerator and the food's about to go bad. It's going to smell terrible. I am not going to stick around to oversee the destruction of the company I love."

Then I told them to shove it and left the meeting. I called Dayna, my assistant, to book me a flight back to Atlanta and went outside to wait for a car to take me to the airport. It was the dead of winter and it was snowing outside, but my blood was boiling. After a couple of minutes, Rick came running out the building with his BlackBerry held high. He handed it to me and said, "Talk."

"Hello?"

"Hey, John, I understand you just told them to shove it." It was Art Williams. Rick had had the presence of mind to call the one person he knew might be able to talk me off the ledge. "Tell me what happened."

I told him what all went down and it was very interesting, because Art's a pretty emotional guy much like myself. When I was finished, he told me, "Hey, John, I remember, I felt that way so many times, but, look: Everything's riding on you. Everybody's counting on you. You can't quit. You've got to go back in there and fight. You've got to go back in there. And if they need to change, you've got to *make* them change."

"All right, I hear you," I said. "I'll go back up and talk to them."

So, while I took a few deep breaths, Rick reconvened everyone in the conference room. I went in and, as calmly as I could, I said, "Look. Y'all can stuff the contract. If you're here to work with us on getting Primerica out of Citigroup—because I'm telling you, you have a melting ice cube on your hands now that you've told us to just quit doing business while we figure this out—I'm here to do that. But I'm not signing anything with you."

After the meeting ended, Citi's CFO at the time, Gary Crittenton, approached us. He told us he understood where we were coming from and admired our commitment to our people. Then, he offered us a potential window to climb through. (Gary is a great example of why it's important not to burn bridges. Today he serves as Lead Director on Primerica's Board of Directors and we have a wonderful relationship.) He referred us to an investment banking firm called Greenhill & Co., Inc. that he thought could help us come up with a deal to bring back to Citigroup. He advised us to come back when it was ready, offer it up, and tell Citi to take it or leave it. He warned, "As crazy as things are here, we might say 'leave it.' But I think the only way you're going to get where you want to get to is to do that."

Talk about high stakes. But, it was a chance.

When Rick and I got back to Atlanta we had a conference call with our top leaders to tell them we had to cancel the Atlantis trip. I was quite emotional, and I think that it was the first time our guys actually realized, *John and Rick are in the middle of a frickin' war.* Then the most amazing thing happened: Even knowing the long odds we were facing and that their own livelihoods were in jeopardy, the good folks on the call told us, "Hey, y'all do what you gotta do. We've got your backs." To say I felt humbled and moved is an understatement.

Fortified in knowing we had the support of our team behind us, we took Gary's advice. We went to Greenhill and, thanks to Rick's genius financial sense, figured out the structure of a deal to take back to Citigroup. Lo and behold, they loved it. The head of Mergers and Acquisitions suggested we do it as an IPO.

We were off and running…. Or, so we thought.

As Rick and I worked toward putting the IPO in place, we hit snag after snag. Every time, Citi would get cold feet and put us back on hold. Naturally, we were getting frustrated with all the stops and starts. I mean, month after month was going by and it was just going back and forth, ad nauseam. By this point, Gary and most of the other Citi executives we knew had been replaced, and the new folks were getting equally frustrated with us. I couldn't blame them, really. Here were these two guys, trying to remove themselves and Primerica from under their control, pretty much acting as regular thorns in their sides. They decided to do a study on what would happen if they just fired us.

Fortunately, we were well-loved within our organization, and people were well aware of everything we had been doing and fighting for on their behalf. When word got around about that study, a plan was hatched. Chess Britt, Primerica's executive VP of marketing and a wise old owl if ever there was one (he even wrote a book called *Seek to Be Wise*), went to Peter Schneider, the company's general counsel at the time (and now president). He suggested that Peter go to New York to personally deliver a presentation on exactly what would happen if Rick and I were to be fired. Together, Peter and his associate general counsel, Alexis Ginn, put together a no-holds-barred presentation to share with the Powers That Be. As Peter went on and on in that conference room, detailing the projections (including actual fire and brimstone), I stood behind him, quietly observing the room. Finally, I put my hand on his shoulder and told him he could stop. By the ashen color of the Citi executives' faces, I could tell they got the message.

Well, mostly.

By the time I got home, my BlackBerry was blowing up because now Citi was leaning toward firing me, Rick, *and* Peter, because obviously he was part of the problem. Luckily, someone on their team still had a shred of sense left, because they asked Alexis to come up for another meeting. Alexis returned to New York to let Citi's execs know that, no, Peter had not been exaggerating in his presentation. Things would actually be *much worse* if we were relieved of our posts. She drove home how important it was to keep current leadership in place and to let us keep doing what we were doing.

I honestly think at that meeting they decided we're all crazy and just gave up. They decided they just needed to get Primerica the heck out of Citigroup. We were allowed to keep going and to persevere, finally achieving our goal of making Primerica its own entity during the IPO on April 1, 2010.

Alexis saved our necks that day, and I am forever grateful to her for that. She will always hold a place in the Primerica Hall of Fame. What made her actions so impressive is how she flipped the script on fear by walking into that room and facing those same people who had our heads on the chopping block just a few days prior. She did it because she was fighting for something much bigger than herself. Winston Churchill talked about what a great gift it is in life to be given the opportunity to fight for a worthy cause. When you're in that position, you must be willing to get uncomfortable. Sometimes that means playing without a net. It took great personal courage for Alexis to march into that board room and do what was required to get the job done in the face of a figurative firing squad.

As I reflect back on that time period, I am struck by how many selfless and dedicated acts of courage went into the making of our IPO, Alexis's visit to Citigroup being but one of them. Rick and I, together with then-president and now CEO Glenn Williams, CFO Alison Rand, Chess, Peter, Alexis, COO Greg Pitts, and so many others, made it through because we were a team. As a team we were a united front with shared goals, a shared vision, and shared determination.

By now, you'll have noticed that I talk a lot about what went on in the war cabinet rooms that Winston Churchill occupied during all of his years at the helm. One thing I don't think I have mentioned, is the sign that Winston had affixed to the desk facing his generals. It was a quote from Queen Victoria that read, "Please understand: There is no depression in this house, and we are not interested in the possibilities of defeat. They do not exist." In other words, he didn't want to hear excuses. He was interested in figuring out what it would take to win.

Churchill himself famously said, "It is not enough to do our best; sometimes we must do what is required."

These quotes resonate with me so strongly because they encapsulate perfectly our team's mindset about getting out of Citibank. A lot of winning and succeeding is just doing what is necessary, no matter how difficult or scary. When Churchill took his position as Prime Minister in 1940, the Second World War was already well underway. One of his first experiences with his new leadership was having them sit in front of him and tell him how they were doing their best, and despite their efforts, it just wasn't working. Well, Alexis Ginn knew what Churchill knew way back then: That our best wasn't good enough. We had to do what was required. And so, she did.

GREY SKIES ARE GOING TO CLEAR UP

When it comes to business and life, there are dark days, and then there are sunny days. Hopefully, you have a lot more sunny days than dark days. That said, when you look back on your career or achievements, you will see it is evident that during the dark days, you earned what you got. After all, it is unlikely you received a huge win or a raise just sitting behind your desk with your heels kicked up, making baskets with wadded-up paper. You might have made it into the top bracket of your office paper basketball team, but that's not the kind of win I'm talking about. Some of your best work has likely been done under the gun, during those dark days, which means you know how to get to work even when you are under pressure.

Weathering the storms that come and go makes those sunny days all the more sweet. Once you start to live this experientially, it can help you flip the script when it comes to living those dark days in the moment. You can be happy for what trials and challenges come your way because you can see them as waypoints, marking opportunities for growth and personal expansion.

I didn't know that my path would look the way it did. Heck, the John Addison from that class in 1975 at the University of Georgia who didn't know what a syllabus was is a very different character than the one who was responsible for Primerica's emancipation.

I didn't just jump from being one person to the next in one big leap, though. I had a lot of failures; trials including lots of error, and room for growth that came my way over and over again. On balance, my path consisted of more dark days than sunny days. Yet, when it was all said and done, I knew that I had given it everything I had and I wouldn't trade any of those dark days. I knew deep down that I had not only done my best, but I had *done what was necessary*. I had faced my fears and overcome them because I didn't give up. No siree. I hung in there until the last moment, until that bell ringing on Wall Street sounded like the Liberty Bell itself. In fact, it was *our* liberty bell.

Here's what I took away from our tumultuous journey to achieve this great success on behalf of our Primerica friends and family: Not walking away is half the battle.

So, in a world where online shopping and fast food, fast coffee, fast relationships, and fast news have created a culture of immediate gratification, how do you cultivate the character necessary to hang in there? Moreover, when you are in the middle of your darkest day, when you're smack in the middle of the trial of your life and you can't see your way clear to the other side, what does it take to be able to stick it out?

The solution to this one resides once again in how you go about perceiving your world. You know the saying, *An ounce of prevention is worth a pound of cure*? Well, what little shift could you make now that will pay off big in the long run?

When you make your goal small acts of success rather than big life achievements, you will start to see that you are a lot more successful than you think. When your idea of what success looks like changes, you begin to realize that success is actually the journey, not the destination. That may not make sense until you sit in it for a while. In fact, it kind of sounds like something that some Zen guy would say. That's not quite me. I am a human becoming, remember; my goose is not fully cooked yet.

What I am (warts and all) is passionate about self-betterment, which means my whole life tends to trend in a direction of betterment. Every time you commit yourself to being just a little bit better every day, even in each new moment, you commit yourself to success. The great thing about this philosophy is you can restart your timer at any time.

Let's say you want to be better than you were yesterday. You wake up on time, get to work early, bring coffee for your boss, get projects handled for most of the morning, have a meeting over lunch, and then you are exhausted by the afternoon. When Sally, the lady whose cubicle is adjacent to yours, asks you if you can get her copies off the machine for her, you give her a look that says, "I'm not your momma. Get them yourself!" while mumbling something similar under your breath. Sally, having worked with you for a few years now, knows that look. In fact, Sally also knows you have been working hard to be more accommodating of others and to give that particular facial expression the old heave-ho. Embarrassed by your attitude, you feel you have failed. What to do?

You consider leaving early, disappearing in a rush, taking the service elevator down so no one will see you on your way out. You could drive home angry, speeding from lane to lane as you berate yourself for not measuring up to your personal standards of perfection that day. Maybe you'd decide to stop at the grocery store for a pint of beer *and* a pint of ice cream in a plan to eat and drink yourself silly so you can forget the lapse in office decorum. Then you'd go to bed hazy, hoping to wake up and do it better tomorrow.

The next morning, you would wake up late because you forgot to set your alarm the night before, with a cloud of alcohol and sugar still swirling around in your brain. Not paying attention in your rush to get dressed, you'd don a wrinkled shirt with a stain. There is no time for coffee, which makes you feel inadequate before the day has even begun. Skidding to a (crooked) stop in your parking spot, you might ding someone's door and guiltily rush toward the office entrance, setting yourself a half-baked mental reminder to come back later and leave a note. When you finally make it to your cube, you would find Sally already at her desk. Because she is generally a friendly, nice person, she would greet you with a warm smile.

Sitting there, diligently typing away and finishing her work early, Sally now represents all your personal and professional failures. Who does she think she is, being so perfect?

Do you see where this is going? Let's rewind to the moment right after you gave Sally "the look." That was the moment you had to make a choice: Tank the rest of the day and continue down a self-sabotaging path—which, we now see, has become a two-day slog—or, stop yourself right then and there after the look. With a simple apology to Sally, you could start your day all over again, right then and there. You could stop the downward trend before it started.

So many people I know live life in terms of days, weeks, months, or even years. I have a friend whose mother always says things like, "I can't wait until next year. This year has been terrible!" She'll say that in April! I don't know about you, but for me, April is number four out of twelve months in the Gregorian calendar. To me, it sounds like she's throwing away eight whole months of potential goodness.

You may be wondering, if we don't live day to day, month to month, or year to year, how *should* we live? Moment to moment. Yes, I also say you should get up and try to be a little bit better today than you were yesterday; but sometimes—and possibly to our ultimate satisfaction—life can be a moment-to-moment game of self-improvement. This means not carrying all those rocks from our past into our present, which consequently affects our future. We start each moment anew. If we fall short, we stop ourselves in that very moment. If we fall short again, well, there's yet another opportunity to do better in each subsequent instant. When you live life that way, you have a whole world of opportunity for growth. The sky truly becomes the limit for what you can achieve, no matter how much fear you face.

LOOKING BACK

Occasionally, when I have time to sit on the porch while the rain falls outside, I like to close my eyes and remember myself back at Casa de Fritos at Six Flags Over Georgia. I can see myself sitting there in that Spanish courtyard, so small, eating my empanadas and thinking I was savoring the world's most exotic cuisine. I remember what a rich experience that was. As growing old has a way of doing to us, for me the magic of that day has dissipated over the years. I know now that you can get empanadas in the local grocery store freezer section. If you had told me that back then, it would have burst my bubble entirely. As an adult, I can see how staged and, dare I say, ordinary (by today's standards) everything there was. I have had more authentic Mexican restaurant experiences at El Sombrero in Gainesville, Georgia. But back then, I did not know any better.

What changed? It certainly wasn't the empanadas; it was my perspective. My perspective changes with the more people I meet, the more food I savor, the more books I read, the more places I travel, and the more conversations I have. Each one of these brings a new understanding, appreciation, and a broader view of what life has to offer. Frankly, it's how I feed myself these days. I like to live on personal expansion (as well as regular veggies from my canning kitchen. Momma always did say, "Johnny, eat your greens!").

If you feel stagnated, stuck, like you're in a dark bog with no hope for a brighter future, it is time for you to pull yourself out of there. You are no good to anyone, let alone yourself, while you are steeped in sadness, fear, or if you're just plain bored to death with the life you've created. If your outlook no longer feels challenged or like nothing in life can get better—or worse—than it is now, it's time to walk out into the sun and, with curiosity, question your own perspective.

11

THE BOUNTIFUL BALANCE

Balance. It's such a beautiful idea. A perfect blend of light and dark. A gymnast poised atop a narrow beam, gracefully completing a series of jumps and flips. A kayaker gliding smoothly over calm water. We all want internal balance as well, and we look for ways to instill more harmony within our lives through meditation or nature or religion. But as beautiful an idea as it is, I have found that balance is mostly just that: an idea. You may define success by living a life in perfect evenness and equanimity, but I see it very differently.

I'd wager a guess that you've noticed how the good times never seem to last as long as the not-so-good times. That you might feel as though you're constantly moving into or out of crisis. You aren't imagining things. That's life! The peaceful, harmonious times should be cherished and appreciated. You should enjoy the dickens out of a good day. Because, more often than not, at any given time the circumstances we face on life's journey are challenging, stimulating, thought-provoking, exciting, patience-testing, or just flat-out hard. (If you find your life to be boring or smooth sailing, then I'd suggest you aren't trying hard enough.) As anyone who has ever attempted to find a quiet spot in a busy airport will tell you, finding so-called "balance" on any given day is tough.

And you know what? I am just fine with this. If you are going to do big things, especially in the leadership world, there are times when your life is going to be in chaos; that is just a fact. Working hard to successfully achieve your goals and dreams necessitates a willingness to be out of balance. You cannot be everywhere at once; you cannot please everyone in your life, simultaneously, all of the time. That just isn't realistic. You can either spend a lot of energy fighting and begrudging the chaos, or you can embrace it.

Now, I'm not suggesting that you forsake your family or children in pursuit of your goals. You absolutely need to spend quality time together; your kids need to be secure in the knowledge that you love them unconditionally. What I mean is, make it one of your goals to be their hero. Model excellence for them and raise them to value achievement. Teach them that the times life will be off-kilter will inevitably outweigh the times when it is even. It is up to us to find a way to enjoy and savor the times when balance does come to call.

As we move further into the concept of balance in our lives, we'll explore the idea that true equilibrium lies not in a static state but in the dynamic interplay between chaos and calm. The journey toward extraordinary accomplishments often involves navigating the extremes, and understanding this interaction between imbalance and stability is yet another key to unlocking your full potential.

AND THIS TOO...

In an old Persian adage handed down and translated time and again over the years, a sultan asked his Eastern sage to find and inscribe on a signet ring a sentiment that would remind him of the perpetual nature and impermanence of life, something true no matter the present conditions. After searching high and low, the sage returned and gifted his sultan the ring. With his head bowed, the sage unfolded the cloth covering the ring to reveal an engraving that said, "And this, too, shall pass away."

You wake up on the right side of the bed, your feet hit the floor, and everything feels good. That good feeling, too, shall pass. You went to lunch with a friend and started feeling sick afterward. That afternoon malaise, too, shall pass. You got a big promotion and are living the high life! That high, too, shall pass. You got fired and your wife left you. That new low, too, shall pass. Can you see where this is going?

Oftentimes, when chaos comes calling, people tend to panic and think they need to do something to fix it, make it better, make the feeling go away. As a kid, if I didn't like something my mom was saying, I'd cover my ears and start humming, "*La, la, la, la, la*" to try to get her to stop talking. As adults, when we hear something or feel something we don't like, we'll take time off, go to a retreat, buy something new, eat junk food, go out dancing, drink wine, stay in bed and binge on television, etc.—basically, anything we can do to avoid discomfort. What we forget in these moments is that life *is* the ups and downs. There's no need to "fix" anything; just keep your focus forward and try not to judge the moment so much. It's just happening. It might feel like it's happening *to* you, but really, life is just happening. And it, too, shall pass. As the saying goes, live every day like it's your last, because one day you'll be right.

MANAGING LIFE'S PARADOXES

Back in 1973, I had a red Ford Maverick. True to its name, the car sometimes felt like it had gone rogue. If I even thought about hitting a curb, pothole, or, some days, just a simple crack in the pavement, the car would begin to wobble and pull. Then, I would have to steer left just to go straight. It was frustrating, but that's life: you have to find your balance in the everchanging imbalance. I always try to remember the old Maverick's message: sometimes, you have to steer left to go straight.

While the common notion of success involves thinking things need to be one way or the other, to be successful we need to embrace both states simultaneously and manage the contradictions of life. For me, this dualism is the space in which internal balance, happiness, and success can be found.

Here's an example of what I mean: In my speeches I will often say, "If you want to succeed, you have to be boldly humble." How do you live life while being bold *and* humble at the same time? Well, some folks are just bold, always thinking they're right and never stopping to listen to anyone else. They charge forward without ever pausing to ask the opinion of others or to take stock of their surroundings. Others are so humble and meek that no one—especially those who have boarded the bold train—would ever hear what they have to say. They almost dissolve into the background, requiring consideration from no one. Neither trait is wrong; they both have their benefits and drawbacks. However, the best leaders I know are those who find ways to integrate the best aspects of both boldness *and* humility.

In a similar vein, it also helps to be confidently unconfident. I hear you. "Really, John?" Yes, really.

If you have all the confidence in the world, you might be quick and overlook a crucial detail, or you might not learn how to ask the right questions. If you are overly confident, you very well might sabotage your own efforts by forgetting to check yourself, ask for help, or listen to those who have ideas better than your own. A little self-doubt can be a valuable trait. Conversely, if you are not confident enough, your ideas and efforts won't go very far. It is likely you will never impact the people you are trying to reach. You can't get anything off the ground without *some* confidence. You have to find a way to integrate confidence with the right amount of self-reflection and questioning. I'll say it again: you have to be confidently unconfident.

You also have to be cautiously aggressive. This one might raise some eyebrows, but hear me out. If you charge into battle without a care in the world, you are likely to get killed. Fear helps keep you alive. However, if you are too cautious and fearful, you'll never even make it to the battlefield. Even worse, you might actually get someone else hurt because of your inability to face the situation. You'll dodge the draft, run for the hills, and not have moved the needle one iota for the troops. The key is being aggressive while still being alert to potential dangers and pitfalls.

That's how you win and that's how you win with fear: you temper it with its opposite. Go ahead and try it out.

As leaders, balancing these opposites, acknowledging and yin and yang of life, and managing the contradictions is the true meaning of a bountiful balance. This dynamic equilibrium fuels the journey to success, where steering left to go straight becomes not only a skill but a guiding philosophy for navigating the twists and turns of leadership and life.

EVERYDAY PHYSICS

I often like to use the lighthouse as a metaphor because it encompasses all the aspects of what real leadership looks like in my mind. But right now, I want you to consider where the lighthouse exists. Perched upon a steadfast foundation, it is surrounded by the crashing waves of a vast sea. Those waves are the lighthouse's constant companion.

As with the ocean, the energy that moves the world—and our very lives—is organized into waves. Some of these waves are visible, like light and water, while other waves, like radio and infrared, can't be seen with the naked eye. Think of these organic waves as a foundation for discerning the rhythms of our own lives. They shape intervals where life envelops us, guiding our encounters and situations through both advantageous and disadvantageous phases.

What we have to remember about waves is that each of them has a crest and a trough.

There is no crashing wave so tall that it has avoided being plunged back into the depths of the sea. That is to say, there are no highs in life without the accompanying lows. There is no emotion without the experience of its opposite—fear included. If we truly visualize the flow of energy all around us and the cycles from which these flows emanate, life's ups and downs become not only understandable but also can be accepted as inevitable. Remember the engraving on the signet ring? And this, too, shall pass away. The lighthouse continues to stand.

With the knowledge that for every high comes an equal and opposite low, we should try to welcome the flux, even when it's uncomfortable. After all, balance is the accumulation of both.

THE SECRET HELP: ADVERSITY

My Cardigan Welsh Corgi, Winston, is one of my favorite furry faces. He will sit and stay if I ask him to (usually). Of course, there have been times he's tucked his tail and run due to sprinkles of rain or a firework popping off in the distance; but for the most part, Winston is more than happy to just sit, stay, and be my buddy.

In life, some people resemble Winston, sitting and staying, waiting for someone to tell them what to do next. I have never been that person. If you have traveled with me, you know that wherever I go, I am going in a hurry. If I get lost, I get lost fast. That's how I find my way even faster!

My adult life has often swung from crest to trough and back again. There have been times I've felt seasick on dry land from all the pitching and hurdling life brought my way. But here's the thing: I would rather be the person who learns how to navigate the ups and downs, the guy who finds a way to keep going despite adversity, than the guy on the beach with his toes in the sand doing nothing for the rest of his life. Regular success tends to breed complacency, and complacency isn't a great initiator of growth. As a servant leader, I am more interested in the growth to be found in the ups and downs.

Scottish essayist, philosopher, and historian Thomas Carlyle said, "Adversity is the diamond dust Heaven polishes its jewels with." Adversity has been a constant companion in my life, and I am grateful for the fact that my life has never just sat and stayed. I have learned so much more about myself and who I am by accepting life's waves as opportunities for growth and embodying the principles of real leadership. In life, if you want to achieve great things, you can't just endure adversity; you have to embrace it as an unparalleled tool for personal expansion.

Lessons, experience, and inherent wisdom all arise from adversity. It's about survival: When you are flung into coping and survival mode, previously unknown strengths and strokes of genius come bubbling up from within. This growth cannot be achieved through simulated adversity. It takes the real world, stress-inducing stuff to bring about the kind of growth I am referring to. So, the next time you see a wave of adversity coming your way, instead of running for shore, you can face it and dive right in, knowing that you are about to be polished to perfection.

I heard something on the radio recently that piqued my interest and feels applicable to this topic; very applicable, in fact. It was a story about two sisters, Corrie and Betsie ten Boom, who were caught and punished for hiding Jewish people during World War II. They were sent to the Ravensbrück concentration camp, where they were located within a female barracks. Close your eyes and remember the conditions in which these people were kept. To say it was inhumane doesn't do it justice. There were toilets in the middle of the room, beds on either side of open waste, no food, little water, and nothing to do all day but either be worked to death or suffer. It was one of the most egregious acts committed against humanity.

Betsie was a mostly positive young lady. She spent her time focusing on helping others within their barracks, praising her Lord, and sharing that faith with others. That was how she passed the time. Her sister, Corrie, had a bit more negative perspective. Who could blame her? She tended to focus on all the suffering, never taking her eyes off of it to see any light. One day, Corrie woke up with fleas. She had finally become infested, and she was relinquishing her desire to survive. Yet, Betsie said they should be grateful for the fleas.

You see, the conditions within the barracks were so deplorable (including the new infestation) that the soldiers who would ordinarily ravage and abuse this female population refused to go inside. This gave Betsie and Corrie time to teach others about the Bible they had smuggled in, to share their faith and improve the mental and spiritual conditions of their fellow prisoners. Had the soldiers been making a regular patrol through their area, the Bible would likely have been found. But because no one wanted to go in, the ten Boom sisters used that hope and the Good Book to inspire other women to fight depression, pray, and have faith in a brighter future. That gave them both purpose and brought the entire community comfort.

Sadly, Betsie died in the camp. However, through a miracle by way of a clerical error, Corrie was released; she went on to share their story of good triumphing over evil thanks to her sister's ability to find strength and hope amidst adversity. Of course, this is an extreme story, but one which bears repeating. Betsie knew how to navigate the negatives, to embrace what she was given, and spin it into gold, even in one of the darkest places on Earth.

Fortunately for all of us, life is a lot easier these days. Bad things certainly happen to good people, but managing how we respond to life's circumstances is ultimately what makes it a win or a loss. You will encounter plenty of people who are searching for a way to stay closer to the midline so they aren't getting tossed from the top to the bottom and back again—maybe you will still catch yourself searching for it from time to time. *But does it exist?* Is there a foolproof way to maintain perfect equanimity in our lives? Or is the concept of a balanced life just as fanciful as dragons guarding towers and rainbows harboring pots of gold at their ends?

BOLSTERING OUR BALANCE

For millennia, people who have suffered the trials and tribulations of life have sought out spiritual answers to their problems of imbalance. I am a big fan of mindfulness, but I don't feel it always has to look like yoga, meditation, or sitting with a guru in the Himalayas.

I garden when I need a balance boost. My hands are in the soil. My knees are on the ground. I am physically closer to the earth. I feel the dirt, roots, and plants. I smell the fresh soil, growing veggies, and budding flowers. The sun is on my skin and I can feel the air all around me, not just because of the humidity (thanks, Georgia), but because I am grounded in my physical reality. When I take time to become part of my environment, it brings me closer to a solid foundation that I can use as a jumping-off point.

I want to look at what gardening is versus what it is not. It isn't me sitting around, just looking at my plants or wishing the blooms would come sooner or be fuller. It isn't me thinking about what I'm going to do next, wondering what might be possible, or lamenting the fact that I chose to plant a hydrangea instead of an iris in the corner. Gardening isn't in my head. It is in the ground, in the soil, in planting, pruning, watering, and taking care of my efforts. Gardening is work. It is peaceful action, and sometimes it takes a lot of effort to keep it all moving forward in the right direction; but to me, it's well worth it.

Even in the pursuit of balance, we can become too cerebral and reflective, which disempowers us to a degree. I'm a man of action. I like getting things done and figuring things out. To be honest, I often figure out what *not* to do before I figure out what to do, which is also okay. The point is, if you spend all of your time thinking about ways to make your life better, to bring it into harmony, you are missing out on the opportunities to take action and make a difference for yourself.

The thing about stability is that it comes and goes. It's a point we pass briefly sometimes as we are on our way into or out of a crisis, and I know this all too well. So, when I am done gardening, I know it is time to reenter the world of imbalance. I'm okay with that because without the noise and chaos of real-world problems, the time spent in my garden is a lot less special. It would be just one more thing added to my to-do list to take up hours of my life instead of functioning as a reprieve. When I think about it that way, the stress, noise, and chaos of the real world become a lot more manageable and not quite as frightening.

I want to highlight a couple of important ideas that can help solidify the everyday application of this concept: First, you can find ways to bring a sense of balance to your life without reaching for something destructive or escapist, like alcohol, gambling, or risky behavior. Spending time in nature is a favorite option for many. Maybe for you it's working on a jigsaw puzzle. The point is to do something that engages the senses and grounds you in the moment. Second, as difficult as it may feel right now, I encourage you to try to find some appreciation for the tumultuous times as compared to more harmonious ones. Imbalance tends to throw us into great fits of fear; but with the right outlook, it doesn't have to.

When I reflect on the dark times in my life—when my momma died, when the future of Primerica was in jeopardy, in the days following my stroke—I remember feeling like there was no way out and nothing I could do would make a bit of difference. I remember how hard some of those times were. My whole outlook was focused very narrowly on this one black cloud that seemed like it settled on me and put everything else into shadow. I could hardly smell the roses, be present enough to enjoy a meal, or see the light. To say they were dark days puts it mildly. Truthfully, sometimes I wondered if things would ever get easier.

Nowadays, life is pretty good. I can sit on my porch, walk through my garden, visit with my grandchildren, and take time to travel. But you know what? Life now is so much more real, so much sweeter and and more vivid because I went through those dark times. I would not be where I am today (or *who* I am today, for that matter) without seemingly endless periods of struggle. Maybe my struggles were long and hard so my relief will be long and easy. I don't know for sure; I just try to live day to day. I don't spend time worrying about life getting hard again and letting that fear steal today from me.

Life will get hard again. I know it will because that's life. As for today, I am going to enjoy my time, because those harder times have made it really easy to appreciate everything I have and everyone I have around me to enjoy life with.

GRANTING FEAR PERMISSION

We have talked about how we can appreciate things more after the dark days, but I know you are still wondering: What about how to get through them? How do I survive when fear is screaming in my face and I don't think I can stand it one more minute?

When I was in the throes of extracting Primerica from Citigroup, my life was riddled with a strong sense of unevenness. Some days, the only time I could take a moment to breathe was in the elevator on the way to a meeting. Every moment was a deluge of thoughts, feelings, fears, and second-guessing myself. I was thinking about everything that was going on and everything I was doing, but I knew I could not let that flood shut me down. Instead, I had to empower myself by acting in spite of the instability and underlying fears.

When I didn't think I could spend one more single second doing what I was doing, I would say to myself, "Okay, I'm gonna stay just one more minute. Then I can leave." I would stay that one minute, and then one more minute after that, and another after that, and so it went.

When I granted myself that freedom, permitting myself to leave after that initial minute, I found myself able to keep pressing on instead. I started by mentally telling the fear, "I hear you, and I hear what you're telling me to do." Then I would push back by responding, "Okay, here's what I *am* going to do." And I'd do it. Usually (but not always), my courage was rewarded with the fear subsiding. Through this practice, I learned that fear could be yammering away in my ear, and I could still plow ahead and handle the things that needed to be handled.

When I learned to respond to fear with action, even if it was only staying one more minute while doing something that needed to be checked off the list, the fear was a lot less compelling than it otherwise might have been.

I believe that action is the greatest cure for fearful inactivity. It's great to have a long-term plan, but you have to win the moment. The more I refused to give in to panic, the more I pressed on by staying one more minute, the more I found myself able to accomplish. All of those minutes added up to heaps of time, making the "impossible" possible.

The truth is that you have loads of strengths that you probably aren't even aware of, but you have to get in the middle of it, in the middle of a catastrophe or crisis, to see those strengths rise and shine. If you never grant the fear permission to be there and stick with it, if you always run away or avoid the challenges in life because they bring up fear, you will miss out on the full range of your capabilities. That would be a darn shame.

12

ACTION THIS DAY

GETTING BEHIND THE PROBLEM

I distinctly remember one evening during the time before Primerica's IPO in 2010. I was in Manhattan, working after hours at my hotel's restaurant. My team and I went there often and the bartender had become a good friend, one who followed our journey from start to finish. On this particular evening, I was beyond tired. The day had become a slurry of words, numbers on pages, lines almost too small to read, noise, bright lights, and ever-changing information. The financial crisis was in full swing, and here I was, trying (very unsuccessfully up until this point) to extract one massive financial institution from another.

I was sitting in my regular spot, which normally would have been a relaxing and welcome reprieve from the day; this evening, it was anything but. All I could hear was too much noise. All I could see was too much motion. All I could feel was the overwhelm of everything around me. It all seemed like too much going on. I had the fleeting desire to stand up and run. Then, I heard the faint sound of soft caroling in the distance.

If you know me at all, you know that Christmas is my favorite time of the year. I put the decorations up early, take them down late, and spend time being holly and jolly as much as I can. This year, I had almost missed it because I was buried in work. I had my head down, nose to the grindstone, almost forgetting what life was about during that time of year. Fortunately, that's not how it unfolded.

This hotel's restaurant was adjacent to the lobby where they had erected their annual Christmas tree. It was enormous, maybe twenty or twenty-five feet tall. This tree was lit from trunk to tip, glowing and shining like the Las Vegas strip.

A group of children had gathered and were filling the resonant chamber of the marble lobby with the sound of youth, hope, and, well, Christmas. At that moment I realized that no matter how Primerica's extraction proceeded, no matter what part I would play in it, and whether or not I would succeed, the world would continue to go on. It was as though the spirit of Christmas had given me an early gift: the gift of perspective. All of a sudden, my visual and perceptual field widened. I could hear everything in the restaurant and nearby areas as though the sound was amplified; but instead of being nerve-jangling, now the sound was crisp and soothing. My focus had shifted from my own internal imbalance to watching life marching on all around me. What a gift that was.

Each conversation became clear, and I could even hear the voices of people seated way in the back of the place. Silverware and glass clinked sharply, the air pressure shifted as doors opened and closed, lights flickered softly, and kitchen staff chattered away as they hurried around in an effort to meet customer demands. Just like when I garden, in a way, I became part of this environment. Somehow, those children and their sweet carols had recentered me and prepared me for the crazy meetings that I would head back into the following day. They had brought me straight into the moment, somewhere I hadn't visited in a long while.

I was grateful.

Grateful for them.

Grateful for the situation.

Grateful for the work.

Every little circumstance and detail of my life, every event, every moment culminated in this one. I could see the path I had taken to get there. It was almost as though my life flashed before my eyes, but something different. It gave everything that had happened in my life—the good and the bad—gravitas and purpose. It was a transformative moment for me going forward. Fear had failed to win again. I had found the *now*. I had come back to reality.

I believe there is a version of ourselves that sits behind the everyday you and me. That version is basically a witness, and that witness spends time watching what is going on rather than acting right away (if ever acting at all). Anytime I am really feeling the hurt, I can tap into that witness and observe myself feeling tired or drained rather than *being the one* feeling tired or drained. No matter what storm I find myself in, I can intentionally pull myself back, get some real-time perspective, and think, *You know what? Compared to what some people deal with, this ain't that big a problem.*

When things get really tough, when I truly have to dig deep, I embrace this idea of mentally stepping back to watch the chaos unfold before me without actually being a part of it. Not only does it offer me the ability to respond to situations rather than react, but it reminds me these are minor blips on the radar of my life. More than that, these blips are the ingredients that make my whole life what it is. These blips make me who I am. How can I resent them? How can I fear them if I know that to be true?

Sitting in that hotel restaurant was the first time I remember taking up temporary residence in the witness part of my brain, where everything became clear, focused, and calm. Despite the whirlwind of activity around me, I felt utterly centered, balanced, and absolutely confident about the effort I needed to put forth to reach our goal of freedom for Primerica.

I used to have a notebook that helped me keep all my scribblings organized. This avoided piles upon piles of papers all askew, with me wondering what I meant by something. Inside that notebook was a sticker that just said FREEDOM on it. Maybe that sticker had finally been absorbed into my subconscious to a great degree. I don't actually know. Sitting in the restaurant that night, I felt with great clarity that no matter what circumstances were swirling around and trying to drown me, that one goal of achieving freedom for my people superseded everything else. I felt like Moses. My inner dialogue was saying, "Let my people GO!" All chaos aside, I felt tremendous confidence in my ability to keep working toward that goal, even if I failed in the end. Heck, by that point, I already *had* failed several times. But I knew that it was my mission, and with that singular mission held inside, I pushed ahead.

What I see in the world is that when people feel an imbalance, when there is pain, frustration, or disorder, that's when they either freeze or flee. That feeling of being off-kilter is so overwhelming and disconcerting that they can't see a way to stay the course and push on. But the truth is, imbalance has nothing to do with whether or not you push on. It's going to occur no matter what. The pushing on is what matters. Observe, find the *now*, and as Susan Jeffers recommends: face fear and keep going anyway.

IMBALANCE AND INACTION

Picture this: Winston Churchill is in the middle of the war. The fate of nations is hanging in the balance. Thousands of people are dying daily at the hands of Nazi Germany. People are scared. Food is being rationed. Folks are starving. Men, women, and children are suffering through life with no hope of an end in sight. There is a pervasive sense of fear and misery. The British nation is preparing to send its sons straight into the battle of a lifetime, and Churchill is once again at the helm, calling the shots.

This particular moment is before the D-Day invasion, and things are relatively calm around British headquarters. The Allies have gotten control of the air and the German bombings have finally ceased. One of Churchill's most promising commanders enters into his office and approaches sheepishly. The commander and his wife have a house in the country, and they wonder if they can just pop away for a quick holiday because they feel that, as far as the command is concerned, nothing big is going on at the moment. With the literal weight of the world on his shoulders, Churchill grins at his commander and says, "Holidays are a peacetime concept."

Churchill is renowned for his productivity. First thing in the morning, he would read the news of the day and conduct correspondence directly from his bed. He'd issue to-dos and orders on stationary with the words ACTION THIS DAY at the top. I think about that phrase and what a true reminder it is to get up every day and get after it. Churchill knew that sometimes you just have to get straight in there, and do what you have to do. This is true, even if you are bored and even if it seems like a weekend when nothing of great significance is happening. There is a job to be done, a fight to win, and someone has got to step in and do it. Someone has got to get after it. If that someone is you, there is no time to sit in the corner and suck your thumb. You have to put on your big boy britches and make it happen.

If you're not already that designated person, but you have the potential to be, keep in mind that leadership often emerges long before anyone formally bestows a title upon you. If you see an opportunity to help others, to be of service, to make a change or a difference for the better, why on earth would you wait for the workweek to start to do something about it? Time is a human construct. There's only now, and now, and now. And then now until infinity. Don't put off until tomorrow what you can get done today. If you wait for a better time to achieve great things, great things will always elude you. Action right now is the key.

Shakespeare's famous play *Henry V* captures a poignant moment highlighting the value of action over inaction. The night before the Battle of Agincourt, Henry can sense the apprehension in his men, so he gives an inspirational speech to rally the troops. He says (in part):

> *This story shall the good man teach his son;*
> *And Crispin Crispian shall ne'er go by,*
> *From this day to the ending of the world,*
> *But we in it shall be remember'd;*
> *We few, we happy few, we band of brothers;*
> *For he to-day that sheds his blood with me*
> *Shall be my brother; be he ne'er so vile,*
> *This day shall gentle his condition....*

During Primerica's exit from Citigroup, our team had to stick together and keep working to accomplish our goals. We became that band of brothers King Henry spoke of. We knew we could rely on one another wholeheartedly. We knew we had each other's backs, no matter what.

When you finally give yourself wholly to accomplishing something of that magnitude, it lives with you forever. It kind of feels like winning a College Football Playoff National Championship, I would imagine. Even when you're up against insurmountable odds, when you face your fears and take action as a collective, you find an opportunity to live beyond yourself, leaving an indelible mark on humanity. That is something special.

If you're the kind of person who falls out of balance and stalls, unable to serve your team, you miss the opportunity to be one of those happy few Henry talks about. You walk alone.

I see plenty of people slow to a stop when things are askew. "I'm going to hold off until I'm out of debt before I make that move across the country." "I'll wait until things around the office settle down before I apply for that promotion." "I'm going to stop smoking when things are a little less stressful." These are real things people have said to me. Do you know what they all have in common? Each one was putting off what could be done now until later. Each one depends on some illusory moment of balance that may or may not come.

This is one of my major frustrations with the mind: it will always try to convince us that there is a better time, one when things won't be as stressful as they are right now, for us to accomplish our goals. But I'll tell you what, moving across the country is stressful. Applying for a promotion is stressful. Quitting smoking is stressful. Our minds will tell us that if we just wait, if we just pause for the clouds to clear, then we can do any of the above without all the stress surrounding it. I don't believe this is true.

Quit putting off living. Quit putting off winning. Quit making excuses, and go make things happen today! None of us is ever promised a single day; you never know when you might run out of tomorrows. Live every day like it's your last, because one of these days you'll be right.

When you are faced with a challenging situation, and your inner voice urges you to back down, give up, or postpone it for later, yet you push forward regardless—that's a sign that fear no longer wields power over you like it once did. This is a big moment! Pause and recognize it. Be proud of yourself. Once you let in the courage it takes to stare fear in the face and deny it, once that courage knows it's stronger than fear, it will start to bubble up from inside you time and time again. The opportunity to embrace it and push forward despite the fear now belongs to you.

All that said, if you find yourself unable to do this immediately, don't be too hard on yourself. Integrating these ideas and concepts into your life can take time. Retraining your mind to respond to fear differently does not happen overnight (or because you read one book). Be patient. Keep an eye out for signs of your progress. When you actively seek opportunities for personal growth, you will find them unfolding before you. I'm sure about that.

ACTION IS THE KEY

I want to make a distinction here. I happen to agree with Churchill's assessment that holidays are a peacetime concept—when we find ourselves in the midst of a prolonged life-changing event, it doesn't behoove us to take our eye off the ball, even during a lull. That said, many of us have yet to see the kind of war in our own lives that Churchill and his peers endured. The challenges we face are not usually of the life-or-death variety; our battlefields tend to be metaphorical rather than literal. But that does not make our Big Goals less scary or overwhelming to our psyche, or less meaningful to our lives, does it? So, while I won't suggest scheduling two weeks on the beach right before you have a career-making presentation coming up is a good idea (*especially* if part of your impetus for the vacation is to avoid thinking about said presentation), I also won't condone ignoring your mental, physical, or relationship health in favor of work. Because if you do that, I guarantee in the end you will lose much more than you might win.

Right now, self-care is one of the hottest topics out there. I am all for it. It's important, after all. Taking vacations, meeting your physical, mental, and spiritual needs, and following the lead of your body are all vital pieces of living a happy and productive life. I spend a lot of my life on my own self-care now, and I would never apologize for it. My health matters to me because I can't make nearly as big an impact if I am unwell.

Many years ago, I had a stroke. It was serious, and it could have put an end to my journey, but I was fortunate that God had further plans for me. During that period, I was under immense stress and pressure; there's no denying that. I was making an effort to carve out time for relaxation, recovery, and personal rejuvenation, enjoying a game of golf on one of Hawaii's most breathtaking courses, when the stroke occurred. Even my dedication to regular vacations and breaks was not enough to keep it from happening. However, that kind of major medical emergency made me take stock of my life: what I was doing with it, where I wanted to go, and how I was going to get there. When I consider it in that light, it was not an unwelcome catastrophe altogether.

That period in my life gave me some great perspective on the topic of balance. I learned then that how I spend my time is more valuable than I ever considered it to be. It reminded me of the truth of my mortality, a truth that would never escape me again. And while I live every single day to the fullest, I also take stock of *how* I live each day to the fullest. Some days, it means gardening or spending time with my grandkids. Other times, it means jet-setting to a foreign location where I might be giving a talk or just relaxing and sightseeing. Still others, it means hours in the office working hard to make sure I leave a legacy behind when I'm called to meet my maker. Moving targets are hard to hit, and I plan on being a moving target until that day, but it doesn't mean I don't rest ... in my own way.

Self-care isn't always about a day at the spa or taking a two-hour bubble bath. Don't get me wrong; sometimes it is. But more often than not, you aren't going to find your balance by scheduling one singular activity into an otherwise packed month of stringent obligations. The truth is that finding your balance is going to be a very individual pursuit, one I can only allude to here due to its highly personal nature. The kind of self-care that brings the most benefit is the type you commit to regularly, not just the kind you desperately grasp for when your level-headed ship is sinking.

Imagine you buy yourself a new truck. It is strong and has the capacity to haul, work long hours, carry a good load of weight and responsibility, and it doesn't complain too much. But how does that truck look five or even ten years from now? Somewhere in between all that hauling, towing, and working, you will hopefully have scheduled a few oil changes and tune-ups, bought some new tires, a new windshield, and maybe every now and then you even put in higher octane than you normally would. Regular maintenance. That's what keeps the truck functional. That's what helps prevent breakdown. You have actively cared for your truck, and so it remains functional longer than it would have otherwise.

I know I'm all about suiting up and showing up, but finding ways to actively care for yourself and enjoy your life while still taking care of professional responsibilities is critically important. The key to it all is action. Action is what moves us through fear when we are certain we can't take another step forward. Action drives progress while allowing fear to fall away. If you need to put some things in place to make sure you have the mental resources available to succeed, then you are acting to preempt the effects of fear, and that is even more effective than waiting to deal with fear when it arises.

THE WAY

No matter your current state or position on the journey toward your goals, you can count on meeting fear along the path. It is a fundamental part of the human experience. Trying to pretend our fears don't exist isn't realistic; nor is it healthy to let fear rule our lives. Left to its own devices, fear can and will steal from us. It can rob us of self-confidence, keep us from taking bold chances, and stop us from living our lives to the fullest. But if we take the time to better understand what we're afraid of, we can make empowered choices about how to proceed.

I often tell folks that, in life, we need to show up and grow up in order to go up. Here's how that applies to fear: When we can recognize fear for what it is—the output of a primitive internal warning system designed to protect us—we can approach it with curiosity, see what it has to say, and *choose to move forward anyway*. There is always a way forward with action.

Action is the catalyst for achievement and advancement, even when that action begins as simple observation. Starting with the smallest step, one minute at a time, you can discover the inner strength to push forward and carve a path toward success. In this moment, you can smile defiantly, savor a quiet revelry, secure in the knowledge that you are turning your fear into the very fuel that will get you where you want to go.

EPILOGUE

For more than twenty-five years, I have used the concept of turning your fear into fuel and not letting your fears be stumbling blocks in my speeches. In fact, this is the story I had in my mind to tell when we published *Real Leadership* in 2016. However, that was soon after Primerica's IPO which, as you've no doubt realized, was a huge deal, and people were eager to hear the details of that triumph. Now, here we are nine years later, and I finally get to put to paper what's been in my heart all this time.

When I first thought to write this book, I was regularly meeting people who were dedicated to their craft or business but who failed to have the self-confidence and courage necessary to make the big moves they wanted to make. It was as though they were standing on one side of a river without a raft, bewildered and forlorn as they stared at the swift water rushing between them and their destination on the opposite shore. No matter how much they wished to get to the other side, they were choosing to wait for a ferry that didn't exist. They didn't see that they were capable of building their *own* raft, fashioning a paddle, donning a life vest, and ferrying themselves across the rushing water. It taxed me greatly to see so many folks stuck, victims of their own inability to act in the face of their fears. I wanted to help.

Then I started thinking, *who am I to write a book about fear?* Seriously, what kind of guy just takes time out of his retirement to write a book on arguably one of the scariest subjects in human history, second probably only to death? Well, how about a guy who has been nearly crippled by fear at times; a guy who, on countless nights, awoke in a dead panic, drenched in sweat, feeling the weight of the world on his shoulders. That's the guy who wrote this book. Afraid as I was, I was a guy who still got out of bed, cleaned himself up, went to work, and got the job done in the end.

I don't experience fear differently than other people. I have simply learned that when fear rises to the surface, no matter how uncomfortable it is, I don't need to pay it too much attention or let it dissuade me from achieving something big.

When I contemplate what determines how well we do in life, I think about how we are all the sum total of our individual life experiences. As the saying goes, we do not choose our parents; the circumstances of our birth are entirely left up to chance. I won the lottery in this regard because I was born to two loving, nurturing, positive parents who always made me feel special and who gave me the emotional and intellectual foundation to succeed in life. I know not all folks have that same advantage. When I ponder the little doubts and demons that are responsible for how well we do out in the world and how we feel about ourselves, very little of where it all originates is within our control. However, we have a lot of control over where we go from there and how we forge our lives. We can buy into the myth that where we come from determines where we'll go and who we will become. Or, we can choose to dream beyond our self-imposed limitations and take the necessary steps to get the job done.

BE THE CHANGE

If there is one thing I have learned about helping people change, it's that, just like Mahatma Gandhi said, you have to be the change you wish to see in the world. If you want your team to be more compassionate, you must demonstrate compassion for them. If you want them to be more generous, you must be generous with them. By that logic, when I wanted to help people be a little bit braver and more courageous, I had to start there, too. What I found then was a roadmap to success for living with and overcoming fear.

I do believe it's possible to eradicate some fears entirely, especially irrational ones. Let's say you have a fear of frogs. You can find ways to be in the same room with them, possibly even hold them or catch them and release them, and get some compassion for those little guys. You can see that they are probably more scared than you are. You hold them in your hands and find that they are not actually going to hurt you at all. However, most fears in life—especially the ones that set us back—are not typically irrational. The ones that scare us stiff are usually the real, rational fears, the ones that bring reality into sharp focus just before it all comes screeching to a halt. *Am I capable? Will I fail? What will happen if I fail? Would anyone love me if they knew the real me? Do I really have the skills to get the job done, or did I just con my way to where I'm at? What if I can't get the job done?*

And then there are the more subtle and insidious fears like, *What if I actually succeed?* Or, *How will my life change when I achieve all my goals? Will I still be in control?* The fearful thoughts around success are the most debilitating, in my opinion, because they are based on a hypothetical reality. If we always block ourselves from achieving a goal due to a fear of being successful, we never have to face it, nor would it be possible; our subconscious knows that is the case. Accepting that fear as truth means staying comfortably underachieving and never facing the scary possibility of success.

Those are the fears running deeper than all the rest, seedlings in our soul that sprout into big ol' weeds if we let them. They block our potential and cause self-sabotaging behavior. They are the ones that will stop us before we even get started—again, *if we let them*. We must be very honest with ourselves about these fears and be on the lookout for them, because they only reveal themselves in very specific ways. One example might be through patterned behaviors that lead to loss after loss due to some circumstance we inevitably create for ourselves. Other people can try to help us see and break these patterns, but they'll only change when we do some serious inner work and get honest with ourselves. We have to recognize and become fully aware of them before we can begin to transform them.

THE SOLUTION IS SIMPLE: DON'T GIVE UP

I don't mean to scare you or give you a sense of doom and gloom here. I want you to be aware of what I know is possible for the human mind to create. I have seen so many attempts by fear to stop me dead in my tracks. There have been times when I have almost been ready to tuck my tail and run the other way because of those voices telling me I couldn't do something—or worse, that I *could* do something, and then my life would spin wildly out of control with more obligations and responsibilities than I could manage. That fear of success is a real thing.

So what's the difference between the man I am and a parallel version of myself who might have experienced the same professional crisis fourteen years ago but chose to take a big payout to cover himself and gone on his merry way? The answer to that is two-fold:

First, I have a sense of dedication to my friends and family at work about whom I care deeply. I knew I couldn't let the company fail and walk away because it wasn't only my caboose on the line. It would have affected thousands of people and their families, causing an endless ripple effect that would permeate the ages of youngsters and their youngsters for generations to come. I don't mean to make myself out to be more important than I am. That's not it. But when you think about how each action you choose is frozen like stones in the annals of time, affecting everything that comes down the line after you, you start to understand how consequential your actions and choices are.

Second, I have confidence in my ability to endure the process of overcoming fear. I can look back on other times in my life when I've faced fears and surmounted them. As Susan Jeffers would put it, I felt the fear and did it anyway. When I feel my confidence waiver and I wonder if perhaps I've finally bitten off more than I can chew, I can look back on past experiences and draw on a reserve of well-earned knowledge that, yes, I am capable of succeeding and I am even capable of navigating that success.

When you distill those two things down to their simplest form, what saved me was having a heart and passion for servant leadership and the courage not to give up. I harbored the knowledge that each river that is hard to cross can, in fact, be crossed. It was up to me to commit to getting in there and doing the work. I was responsible for getting to the other side.

I am going to leave you with one final quote. I have shared many with you throughout this book, but this one is perhaps the most impactful, even in its simplicity. One of my personal heroes, Vince Lombardi, once said, "Winners never quit, and quitters never win." That's really what it all boils down to, isn't it?

So whatever it is you want to achieve, if you are experiencing fear, and even if you let that fear stop you for a short while, take some deep breaths and get back in the game. The only time we lose is when we let fear convince us to quit altogether, and I know in my heart of hearts that no one reading these words is a quitter.

If you were, you wouldn't have gotten this far, and you wouldn't be invested in trying. So, I can say with great certainty that you already have what it takes to turn your fear into fuel.

I'll see you at the top because the bottom sure is crowded.

ABOUT THE AUTHOR

John Addison, former co-CEO of Primerica, is a world-class motivational speaker and consultant who believes real leadership is one of the world's scarcest resources. As the founder of Addison Leadership Group, Inc., John is helping people across the world with their personal growth. "You're either green and growing or ripe and rotten," John likes to say, as he utilizes over four decades of stories from his own life to encourage people to embrace leadership as a service to others rather than simply a title. He is the author of *Real Leadership: 9 Simple Practices for Leading and Living With Purpose*, a *Wall Street Journal* and *USA Today* bestseller, and *Addisonisms: Quotes to Live By*.

MISSION LEADERSHIP

John is the creator of the Mission Leadership Academy, an online, nine-module course designed to reach and empower people right where they are. Mission Leadership promotes curiosity, positivity, and humility as it asks leaders to look honestly at their strengths and weaknesses. If you believe that there's no higher calling than service to others, join the #MissionLeadership movement today!

The Academy offers the tools needed for people to move forward with confidence as they navigate themselves and others from the lowest valleys to the highest mountains.

Over the course of nine modules, participants learn about effective communication, the true power of trust and inspiration, how to navigate even the hardest things in life, and what to do when life feels impossible. If you are ready to approach life head-on and help others plot their own maps to their best futures, sign up for the FREE Mission Leadership Academy course today.

Join John Online

facebook.com/JohnAddisonLeadership
instagram.com/addisonleadership
linkedin.com/in/johnaddisonleadership

Made in the USA
Monee, IL
14 April 2025

16879ae0-ca11-43bf-b3ac-0e0ec4378a2cR02